MRS CHIPPY'S LAST EXPEDITION

MRS CHIPPY'S LAST EXPEDITION

The Remarkable Journal of
Shackleton's Polar-Bound Cat

COMPLETE AND UNABRIDGED

CAROLINE ALEXANDER

With an Introduction by
Lord Mouser-Hunt, F.R.G.S.

BLOOMSBURY

Grateful acknowledgement is made to
the Royal Geographical Society, London; the
Scott Polar Research Institute, Cambridge; and the
Dulwich College Archives, copyright holders, for
permission to reproduce drawings and photographs
in their collections.

First published in Great Britain 1997
Bloomsbury Publishing Plc,
38 Soho Square, London WIV 5DF

A CIP record for this book is available
from the British Library

ISBN 0 7475 3527 2

10 9 8 7 6 5 4 3

Typeset in Great Britain by
Hewer Text Composition Services, Edinburgh
Printed in Great Britain by
St Edmundsbury Press Ltd, Suffolk

Photographs by Frank Hurley

*Drawings by W. E. How, Able Seaman,
who served on the* Endurance

To little Mango
Ndikupezani

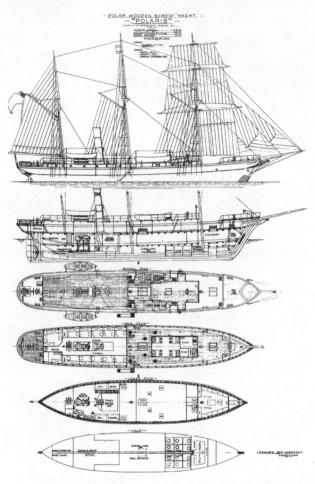

Shipwright's blueprint of the Endurance, *detailing passageways and areas used by Mrs Chippy.*

Introduction

If one were inclined to ask the explorers of our own era to identify those individuals whom they regarded as their most exceptional predecessors and whom they credited with most inspiring their own endeavours, it is an undoubted fact that Mrs Chippy's name would appear near the top of every list. Belonging to the heroic age of exploration that ended with the First World War, Mrs Chippy will ever remain the explorer's Explorer.

The stirring story of this remarkable polar hero is well known. Recruited to accompany Sir Ernest Shackleton on his 1914 Expedition to Antarctica, Mrs Chippy endured almost a year of unimaginable privation and hardship when the Expedition was shipwrecked in the icy wastes of the Weddell Sea. The story of how this remarkable explorer endured the iron paw of Nature is one of the very greatest records of heroic achievement, of any age.

Mrs Chippy hailed from the small village of Cathcart, outside Glasgow, and was a mate of Henry 'Chippy' McNeish, a carpenter and master shipwright who also sailed with Shackleton on the ill-fated *Endurance* expedition. A tiger-striped Tabby with dramatic dark markings, Mrs Chippy would have cut a striking figure in places less glamorous than a polar-bound expedition. Solidly built, with a frank, broad face and handsome whiskers, Chippy inspired instant trust and affection in all he met. The name 'Mrs Chippy' was mistakenly bestowed by his shipmates, beguiled by the playful and charming aspects of his character. Even after the foolish error was determined, the affectionate name stuck and it is a tribute to Chippy's rugged masculinity that he remained unperturbed by this comic misapprehension.

According to Sir Ernest Shackleton, 'the qualities . . . necessary to the explorer are . . . first, optimism; second, patience; third, physical endurance.' These were qualities Mrs Chippy possessed in abundance. While his shipmates fretted anxiously about their safe return to their homes, Mrs Chippy greeted each new dawn with complacent optimism, often sleeping patiently through the winter days. A champion mouser, Chippy was additionally blessed with both agility and stamina, physical traits that served him well in his long ordeal.

The *Endurance* had sailed from London's East India Docks on August 1, 1914, bound for the Antarctic. Ports of call were made at Plymouth, Madeira, Tenerife, and Buenos Aires before heading for South Georgia Island, the most remote outpost of Britain's empire. Here, the *Endurance* passed a month, making scientific investigations and gathering valuable intelligence from the sea-hardened

Norwegian whalers who were the island's chief inhabitants. Here, too, the *Endurance* embarked its last passengers, two pigs (named Patrick Dennis and Lady Bridget Dennis) taken on board to be used later as bacon.[1]

At last, on December 5, 1914, the *Endurance* left the small whaling station at Grytviken and began its journey South.

The objective of the Imperial Trans-Antarctic Expedition led by Sir Ernest Shackleton was nothing less than the crossing of the Antarctic continent – from Vahsel Bay, on the icy shores of the Weddell Sea, over barrier ice, glaciers, crevasses and snow drifts to the Ross Sea, fifteen hundred miles away. Only three years earlier, the famous Norwegian explorer Roald Amundsen had won the race to lead the first team to the South Pole. Crossing the ice-bound continent from sea to sea was the last great prize in polar exploration – indeed, the last great prize of exploration in any quarter of the globe.

This was Shackleton's third Antarctic expedition. His second, conducted in 1907–1909, when he had led a team to within one hundred miles of the South

---

[1] Interestingly, Mrs Chippy makes no mention of the pigs in the Journal. Thomas Orde-Lees, however, remarks in his diary that Mrs Chippy was 'very funny with the pig' and 'couldn't make him out at all' (T. H. Orde-Lees, diary, 21 November 1914). Lees's entry is characteristically flawed (one is hard pressed to believe that a knowledgeable and worldly seaman like Mrs Chippy could not 'make out' a pig!), yet it has undoubtedly preserved an element of truth. It is safe to conclude that the pigs held no interest for Mrs Chippy.

Pole – the Farthest South at that time – had made him a national hero. A few of the *Endurance*'s crew had accompanied him on this earlier expedition, while the majority, like Mrs Chippy, were shipping with him for the first time. Shackleton's method of recruitment was entirely personal: he simply chose persons whom he felt he could trust and whom he liked. Past qualifications did not count so much as character. Shackleton's eye had fallen approvingly on Mrs Chippy, in whose frank and open countenance he had discerned the ideal shipmate. At the same time it should be noted that Mrs Chippy possessed qualities and experiences that peculiarly suited him, perhaps as much as any member of the crew, to the hazards of polar exploration. A native of Scotland, he was hardy and well conditioned to extremes of inclement weather. His years in the shipyards and carpenters' shops had taught him much about the technical side of sailing, and he was as much at home amid the noisy confusion of tangled masts and yardarms as in a cosy cabin.

The Imperial Trans-Antarctic Expedition was twenty-nine in number. This included Shackleton, the Skipper of the *Endurance*, the navigator, carpenter, carpenter's mate, photographer, scientists, engineers, surgeons and sailors; and a twenty-year-old British stowaway who joined the ship in Buenos Aires and whom Mrs Chippy, perhaps pitying his youth and relative inexperience, particularly befriended. Also taken on board were a motley collection of sixty-nine Canadian husky dogs, purportedly to be used for sledging

Mrs Chippy and Perce Blackborow, the stowaway.

purposes. As matters turned out, they fulfilled no useful tasks to speak of and represented a costly waste of meat and, requiring as they did constant attention, manpower. Mrs Chippy's misgivings at the start about the wisdom of including dogs in an undertaking of this kind were to prove all too justified.

The *Endurance* itself was a barkentine, a three-masted sailing vessel, with the foremast square-rigged and the others rigged fore and aft. It was also equipped with a 350-horsepower steam engine, fired by coal (and, when this supply had been exhausted, by seal blubber), a necessity for negotiating the icy labyrinth of the polar seas. The fate of this beautiful craft – the last of her kind ever built by Norway's famous Framnaes shipyard – marks the beginning of the ordeal for Mrs Chippy and the other expedition members. On January 19, 1915, at position lat. 76°34'S, long. 31°30'W, well into the treacherous Weddell Sea and less than eighty miles from its destination, the *Endurance* was trapped in ice, 'frozen,' as the ship's storekeeper wrote, 'like an almond in a piece of toffee.'

For close to ten months, Shackleton and his men were held captive in the ice-bound *Endurance*. As long as the boat withstood the pressure of the icy pack, the crew were safe. But towards the end of July 1915, the ice began to tighten its cruel grip in earnest, eventually crushing the gallant *Endurance* like an eggshell. Shackleton gave orders to abandon ship and the Imperial Trans-Antarctic Expedition was stranded on the fickle ice.

At the heart of the story of the Expedition's struggle to survive in the polar wastelands lies Mrs Chippy's saga – a saga of physical endurance to be sure, but above all else a lesson in heroism of the highest moral order. And it is one of the rare and happier accidents of History that a record of this saga was left by Mrs Chippy himself, whose Journal of his polar adventures has long been regarded by those who knew of it as a Classic of its kind. Up until the present time, however, interested scholars and readers have had to rely on the original weather-beaten manuscript (housed in the Scottish Geographical Society archives), or the lengthy but disjointed excerpts published in Heinrich Furrer's anthology of polar exploration. The present edition, long overdue, represents Mrs Chippy's entire Journal, complete and unabridged, and annotated with helpful footnotes.

A word should be said about the text itself. Like other great epics, the Journal begins in medias res. The loss of Mrs Chippy's account of the early stages of the Expedition – whether because such an account was materially lost, or because it was never written – has been long lamented by historians and explorers. The heady send-off from the London docks, the swiftly covered miles of open sea, the first glimpse of Antarctica's winter Fairyland – these are the lost scenes that will always tease the imagination.

Occasionally, a fortuitous cross-reference from the diary of another member of the Expedition rewards one with a privileged glimpse of this earlier period. One dramatic example will suffice. On the night of 13 September, 1914, as the *Endurance* headed South, one of Mrs Chippy's shipmates made the following chilling entry: 'An extraordinary thing happened during the night. The tabby cat – Mrs Chippy – jumped overboard through one of the cabin port holes and the officer on watch Lt. Hudson, heard her [sic] screams and turned the ship smartly round & picked her up. [Mrs Chippy] must have been in the water 10 minutes or more.' (T. H. Orde-Lees, diary, 13 September 1914). Fortunately it was a calm, still night when this terrifying incident occurred. This being said, there can be no question that a less redoubtable and level-headed Explorer – an Explorer without the presence of mind to boldly summon assistance while all but engulfed in the inky night waters of the South Atlantic – would have met with inescapable Tragedy. The reader must continually bear in mind that the Journal, for all its richness, represents but a narrow slice of an already full and heroic life, and undoubtedly much else remains untold. Similarly unfortunate is the Journal's famous problematic ending, which has distressed more than one generation of scholars.

As it is, the Journal's first entry is dated January 15, 1915, some five months after the *Endurance* had left its London dock, and only days before it became trapped in the treacherous ice. The *Endurance* entered the dangerously ice-strewn waters on January 18, and for six days afterwards a northeasterly gale raged, compressing the loose 'brash' against the

Antarctic continent. While unable to move within this tightly packed sea of ice, the *Endurance* crew nonetheless hoped, and indeed initially expected, that the following winds and currents would eventually break up the pack, allowing them to sail to freedom. When this expectation was not met, they resorted to attempts to cut and saw the ship from the ice – puny, ineffectual attempts that were mocked by the icy face of unconquerable Nature.

The conclusion of this epic, although not covered by the Journal, is well known: after many months of hardship on the ice floes and high seas, Shackleton accomplished the rescue of the expedition – and lost not a man.

What prompted Mrs Chippy to leave the comforts of home for the unknown rigours of a Polar Expedition? The inner workings of the minds and spirits of the truly great must always remain mysterious to those of us who are left behind. A single entry in Mrs Chippy's Journal brings us, perhaps, as close as we will come to understanding such singular motivation. Contemplating the Antarctic ice fields one night under the light of a luminous full moon, Mrs Chippy deftly likens the snowy hills and hummocks to shining peaks of whipped cream. The Journal's brief entry on this day is eloquent: 'Reflected that only Explorers witness such sights.'

LORD MOUSER-HUNT, F.R.G.S.
PUDDLEBY-ON-THE-MARSH

MRS CHIPPY'S
LAST EXPEDITION

Some of Mrs Chippy's shipmates and fellow Expedition members at the outset of the Expedition.

Mrs Chippy's *Endurance* Journal

Members of the Imperial Trans-Antarctic Expedition

SIR ERNEST SHACKLETON	leader
FRANK WILD	second-in-command
FRANK WORSLEY	captain
LIONEL GREENSTREET	first officer
HUBERT T. HUDSON	navigator
THOMAS CREAN	second officer
ALFRED CHEETHAM	third officer
LOUIS RICKINSON	first engineer
A. J. KERR	second engineer
DR ALEXANDER H. MACKLIN	surgeon
DR JAMES A. MCILROY	surgeon
JAMES M. WORDIE	geologist
LEONARD D. A. HUSSEY	meteorologist
REGINALD W. JAMES	physicist
ROBERT S. CLARK	biologist
JAMES FRANCIS HURLEY	official photographer
GEORGE E. MARSTON	official artist
THOMAS ORDE-LEES	motor expert and storekeeper
HENRY MCNEISH	carpenter
MRS CHIPPY	carpenter's mate
CHARLES J. GREEN	cook
WALTER E. HOW	able seaman
WILLIAM BAKEWELL	able seaman
TIMOTHY MCCARTHY	able seaman
THOMAS MCLEOD	able seaman
JOHN VINCENT	able seaman
ERNEST HOLNESS	fireman
WILLIAM STEVENSON	fireman
PERCE BLACKBOROW	stowaway (later steward)

January 15th. A rather breezy day. Breakfast of tinned rabbit waiting for me in my bowl. Went on deck for my Watch, stationing myself under stern rail and leaning over so as to observe the bubbles in our wake. Was joined at rail by some of my shipmates, all commenting on our excellent progress. 'So, Chippy,' said Hussey, 'it's nice to be on the move again, with the wind in your whiskers, eh?' 'Mind, now,' said Cheetham, 'you don't want to interfere with Mrs Chippy's intensive study of the high seas.'[2] I enjoy it when we are well under way, even though it means a lot more work for me. As Cheetham appreciated, my Watch today was very strenuous, it being extremely difficult to concentrate on all the kinds of movements,

[2]Leonard Hussey was the Expedition's meteorologist. He was well liked for his sense of humour and his banjo playing, with which he entertained Mrs Chippy and other members of the crew. Alf Cheetham was the ship's Third Officer. Captain Frank Worsley (see below) was affectionately known as 'the Skipper.'

ripples, running water, bubbles, froth, foam, etc.,
let alone look out for penguins that might be
following in our wake. Continued to make
nautical observations until teatime, which I took
with my shipmates below. 'Well, we made a
good run of it today,' said the Skipper, while
we had our tea. 'And I saw Chippy was on the job
again, so things must be looking up.' My shipmates are in high spirits, although I was a bit
worn out. I am the only one who takes that
particular watch station, so it is rather a strain.
And it is only one of my many duties.[3]

January 16th. Stern watch cancelled on account of
no movement at all today.[4] Continued my duties
below in boiler room, waking just before teatime.
Joined my shipmates in the wardroom, where

---

[3]Monitoring the *Endurance*'s wake was a critical task, the wake
being of course a mark of the ship's progress. The *Endurance* had
broken through the main pack of ice on 9 January, since which
time she had enjoyed generally good sailing conditions. However, troublesome signs of ice were reappearing and on 14
January, the day before this entry, the path of the *Endurance* had
been blocked by ice that prohibited her moving at all that day.
Mrs Chippy and the other members of the Expedition were
therefore glad to be under way again.

[4]In fact the Skipper's Log records that the *Endurance* had made
excellent progress throughout the night of 15 January and well
into the following morning (124 miles in twenty-four hours),
being brought to a halt only at 8:30 A.M. on the morning of the
sixteenth, by the reappearance of heavy pack ice. Mrs Chippy's
watches, however, generally began some time after noon, a fact
that accounts for this inconsequential error in the Journal.

Wordie had spread some new specimens, i.e., iceberg lumps, on one of the tables. We are a proper Expedition, of course, which means we don't just explore, but also do work important to Science, collecting rocks, lumps, gravel and so forth, as well as Biological specimens, to which I occasionally contribute. Joined my colleagues at the table to conduct a brief investigation of the specimens with the tip of my paw, observing range and types of movement, etc., both on the table and then on the floor. 'I see Mrs Chippy's analysing the effects of gravity again,' said James to Wordie, as I leaned over the edge of the table to observe the progress of one of the specimens as it rolled in a very satisfactory manner under the table.[5] 'I hope you're recording the results,' he said. 'Oh yes,' said Wordie, 'I keep a special file on Chippy's various contributions.' This was exceedingly gratifying to learn, as I don't really have occasion to write up reports and so forth, on top of my many nautical duties. Wordie was just reaching down to retrieve the lump when old Lees spoke up from one of the other tables, where he had been pretending to read his book. 'So Chippy's allowed on the tables, now?' he asked in his peevish voice. My shipmates all stopped what they were doing and looked at him. 'Well,' said Wordie, slowly. 'I don't see the harm in it.' Lees

[5]Reginald James was the Expedition's physicist; James Wordie was the geologist and magnetician.

rolled his eyes in a rude way and went back to pretending to read his book. My shipmates looked at each other and started to laugh. Lee is not at all scientifically minded and is completely out of his element when it comes to these kinds of professional exchanges.[6]

January 17th. Up early a little past noon, joining my shipmates on deck for First Watch. Found everyone gathered at the rails, grumbling and growling about the ice.[7] On days when we don't move everyone is very dull and preoccupied, and not at all social. Cancelled aft watch on account of there being no wake and also a lot of snow blowing, and determined to finish my duties below.[8] Was distracted by the dogs' rude, uncouth barking and decided to take a shortcut across their roofs, just to update myself on their situation. Nimbly jumping up, I strolled across the line of kennels, stopping midway to sniff the air and take in the view. What a lot of noise! My word, these dogs are very un-seamanlike! Was casually cleaning my whiskers on top of the

[6]Thomas Orde-Lees, a so-called motor expert and later storekeeper, was perhaps the most disliked individual on the Expedition. Standing apart from his shipmates, he was the butt of many jokes and unlike Mrs Chippy made no friends.
[7]'Growl and go' was the unwritten code of the British seaman.
[8]Mrs Chippy routinely monitored the ship's furnaces and stoves. The reader is quickly impressed with the extraordinary range of duties recorded by the Journal.

An iceberg typical of those seen by Mrs Chippy.

middle kennel when I was joined by Blackborow.[9] 'What have you been up to now, Mrs Chips?' he said. He leaned across the kennel top to rub my head. 'Poor doggies,' he said, laughing. Blackborow is a good sort, so I let him rub my head and stroke my shoulders. 'Come on,' he said, 'before you get into trouble.' I noted that Macklin was running over to see what the commotion was all about and as I'd finished my watch I let Blackborow accompany me inside on his shoulder. This fretting about the dogs 'losing condition' is all a lot of nonsense.[10] There is nothing wrong with them that an honest day's work wouldn't cure. Now that they've stopped being seasick, all they do is lie around all day eating and making a lot of noise, which comes of them having been assigned no specific Duties like the proper members of our Expedition. Watched over Blackborow's shoulder as Macklin lay into

[9]The kennels stood fore and aft, along the port and starboard sides of the main deck. Here the sledging dogs were housed, confined by stout chains. Dr Alexander Macklin (see below), one of the ship's two surgeons, had the unpleasant task of overseeing the troublesome animals. A number of Mrs Chippy's shipmates refer in their diaries to the 'wolfish wail' that daily rose from the kennels at sundown. Perce Blackborow was the young stowaway who had been made ship's steward, and was a special friend of Mrs Chippy. Among other critical duties, he was responsible for the maintenance of Mrs Chippy's bowl in the galley.

[10]Shackleton notes in his diary that he was concerned about the condition of the dogs, as they had received no exercise at all since early January, when they had been put through their paces on the solid pack. Evidently he had mentioned this concern within Mrs Chippy's hearing.

them, cuffing them into order. To bed early between my mate's ankles.[11]

January 18th. Enjoyed a pleasant afternoon on deck with my shipmates watching for ice and growlers.[12] Everyone has been complaining about the ice and how slowly we are going and how we didn't move at all yesterday etc. etc., but in fact this is much steadier and less strenuous and also allows better observation, i.e., of seals. Observed as the big topsail was unfurled, all crackling and rippling in the wind, while Cheetham raised the chanty for the sailors. Joined the Skipper at my stern watch, looking over the side from under the rail, ears and whiskers forward, attention firmly on the bubbles and other movement. 'Careful now, careful!' the Skipper kept calling out. 'Easy with the rudder.'[13] Continued to look intently over the

[11]Henry 'Chips' McNeish, an old Dundee salt, was Mrs Chippy's mate and the ship's carpenter. Early the following morning, the gale dropped, allowing the *Endurance* to proceed under sail down a lane that had opened in the ice. By this time, however, Mrs Chippy was in bed asleep.

[12]Technically, 'growlers' are relatively small, greenish pieces of sea ice that barely show above water level, and are therefore treacherous to boat navigation. Mrs Chippy, however, shows a marked fondness for the word and frequently employs it to refer to a variety of types of ice.

[13]The ship's rudder and engine propellers were vulnerable to damage by the ice, and consequently were carefully monitored. The prevalence of ice on this day prompted Shackleton to safeguard the propellers by cutting the *Endurance*'s engines and proceeding under sail.

Into the sea of ice.

rail, observing growlers and water, leaning forward – 'Chippy!' said the Skipper suddenly; then called out, 'I think it might be wise if someone were to relieve Mrs Chippy of this somewhat slippery watch.' 'Come on,' said Bakewell, stepping forward and scooping me up. 'It wouldn't do to have the First Mate tumble overboard again.'[14] Accompanied Bakewell under his arm to the main hatch, then went below for tea. The Skipper knows how demanding that particular watch station is, and knows, too, how I tend to overextend myself in my duties. Enjoyed a little snooze in the wardroom after tea, listening to my shipmates discuss the ice and Conditions. 'The character of the ice has changed,' said the Boss.[15] 'Yes,' said the skipper. 'It's like sailing into a pudding.' A splendid conclusion to our day.

January 19th. Slept rather later than usual, on account of night duties. Awoke before midnight and went up top to join my shipmates on deck, where I found them leaning over the port rail, looking at the ice.[16] 'Here's your mate,' said

[14]Able seaman William Bakewell, the only American on the *Endurance*, was the mate of Mrs Chippy's special friend Blackborow. His words here undoubtedly refer to the horrifying incident discussed earlier (see Introduction, page 8).

[15]The crew's affectionate – and respectful – name for Shackleton.

[16]Mrs Chippy is writing during the Antarctic summer, of course, during which time the expedition enjoyed nearly twenty-four hours of sunlight a day, the sun setting briefly

McLeod to my mate as I greeted them, rubbing against their big boots. 'Chippy, you could have saved yourself a trip,' said my mate. 'There's nothing happening here worth looking at,' he said, picking me up and placing me beside him on the rail. 'Stuck fast!' he said, in his growly voice.[17] Observed the ice all shining around us, very splendid in the light. It looks nothing at all like a pudding.[18] Noted the Boss and Skipper on the bridge, but knew from the way their silhouettes were all hunched over and preoccupied that they would not be very social, so joined my mate when he turned in. Bunked between his ankles.

---

only around midnight. This evening of 18 January was to be memorable for the Expedition; while making her way towards open water between two large ice floes, the *Endurance* had entered loose 'brash' ice, which had proven extremely difficult to navigate. A decision was made, therefore, to lie to until a change in the direction of the wind opened the ice up again. This proved to be a fateful decision. Instead of opening, the ice closed decisively around the ship during the night, prohibiting all movement. The night of 18 January, then, can be fairly said to mark the beginning of Mrs Chippy's long ordeal.

[17]McNeish's Scottish burr was described by a fellow shipmate as rasping 'like frayed wire cable' (G. Bowman, *Men of Antarctica*, p. 72). By contrast, Mrs Chippy refers to his rough voice with evident affection.

[18]Worsley's choice of expression was misleading. By likening the ice to a 'pudding' he had been referring to its slushy, soupy consistency and dangerous tendency to close in around the ship. Mrs Chippy was surely not alone in interpreting his words to mean something rather more pleasant.

January 20th. Frozen seal for breakfast. Stern watch cancelled on account of there being no wake.[19] Seal for lunch, and also for dinner. To bed early, then up again near midnight for night Duties. Reexamined bowl just in cast Blackborow had added a little something before going to bed, although this turned out not to be the case. Made a very profitable trip down to the hold for some mousing.[20] Obtained two excellent specimens and decided to make a gift of one of them to my shipmates on Night Watch. Walking softly up the stairs and along the passage, I found Cheetham warming his feet by the watch stove, with his head in his hands, looking very glum.[21] Called by mewing to indicate I had arrived with a present, and carefully presented him with the mouse.

---

[19]Shackleton wrote that 'a survey of [our] position on the 20th showed that the ship was firmly beset. The ice was packed heavily and firmly all round the *Endurance* in every direction . . .' (Shackleton, *South*, p. 30). Heartbreakingly, the *Endurance* was only some eighty miles from her destination, Vahsel Bay. It is in this time of increasing crisis that the mettle of Mrs Chippy's character is memorably displayed: it is a striking fact that of all the accounts left by Expedition members, Mrs Chippy's Journal is the *only* one to relate the events of these telling days without a trace of anxiety. Indeed, Mrs Chippy scarcely mentions the ice conditions at all.

[20]Mrs Chippy was an enthusiastic amateur naturalist.

[21]Alf Cheetham was a veteran of Antarctic exploration and knew as well as anyone the dangers presented by the close-packed ice to the *Endurance*. Mrs Chippy evidently encountered him in a low moment; as becomes increasingly evident, few members of the Expedition possessed Mrs Chippy's deep reserves of moral strength.

'Good Lord, Chippy!' he said, jumping as I laid it by his feet. 'Is this for me?' Indicated to him some of the various sorts of ways a mouse can work with a few demonstrative tosses and so forth. Cheetham began to laugh. 'Good old Chippy,' he said, and brought me on to his lap for a little comradely socializing. 'It's been a long, wretched night, and this is just what the doctor ordered,' he said. Settled purring on his lap, becoming quite toasty from the fire. Somehow I must have dozed off, because I woke to find myself on Cheetham's sweater and Crean stoking the stove. Rechecked my bowl then joined my mate on his bunk. These night watches certainly take their toll, and are part of what makes a sailor's life so difficult.

January 21st. Stern watch cancelled on account of no wake. Our ship's rudder was all frozen in the ice, requiring some of my shipmates to go overboard and cut it free. This is the kind of job for specialists, not requiring my attention, and also it was rather cold, so concluded my watch and went below to spend the rest of the day on duty in the galley and wardroom. Was woken by my shipmates when they all came stomping in with their big sea boots. 'Time for tea, Mrs Chippy,' said Crean, as Blackborow and Cookie came in with all the mugs and plates and teapots.[22] Suddenly Lees

[22]Tom Crean, the second officer, was a hardy, experienced Antarctic explorer.

approached the table, looking all pink and pinched. 'I thought Mrs Chippy wasn't supposed to be in the wardroom,' he said in his peevish voice. 'I thought that was the whole point of that meeting.' Lees is so very antisocial I wonder that he manages to get on with my other shipmates at all. Firstly, it was hardly a 'meeting,' only a little conference. Something or other was said to the effect that my duties would possibly mostly lie in my mate's cabin and the galley, but that's the sort of thing people say all the time without thinking things through properly. It was all some time ago, anyway, before everything settled down and the nature of everyone's duties was established, and I never paid it any attention. With his earmuffs and pink nose Lees looks like a mouse.[23] 'I thought it had been absolutely decided,' he began again, in his whiny voice. 'Go on with you,' said Cheetham to Lees, angrily. 'What does it matter to you where Mrs Chippy goes? Besides,' he said, rumpling my fur in a comradely way, 'Chippy's better company than some I know who use the wardroom.' My shipmates laughed while Lees got pinker. 'What's the point of making rules if they're only going to be broken?' he said in his whiny voice above my shipmates' laughter. 'First it was the galley, then the cabins, and now it's even the wardroom tables!' I stretched and yawned; then stood up and arched my back

[23]See the photograph on page 18.

Thomas Hans Orde-Lees.

before resettling on the table, indicating I was ready for my tea. Just then the Boss came in. 'Tea ready?' he asked, and while Blackborow brought him his mug I jumped down and greeted him respectfully, rubbing against his boots. 'Hell-o, Chippy!' he said very heartily, bending down to stroke me. 'What have you got to report from the stern watch today?' Old Lees went off into a corner on his own to pretend to read a book, while I accompanied Sir Ernest to his chair in order to thoroughly brief him on my Watch.

January 25th. Rudely awoken by the engines rumbling and everything shaking. Found my breakfast bowl rather hastily filled, not topped up properly like Blackborow usually does it. Lots of confusion and running around on deck, sails flapping, dogs yowling, etc. etc.[24] Found my stern watch station crowded with a number of my shipmates hanging over the side, blocking my way and making it very difficult to get to my job. Manoeuvred between Cheetham's and Bakewell's boots and observed our ship propeller churning splendidly, making a lot of splash and froth. Was almost stepped on by Marston, who has no business

---

[24]A crack in the ice as much as a quarter of a mile wide and a mile long had appeared in the night some fifty yards ahead of the ship. By summoning every ounce of engine and sail power, Shackleton hoped to force the ship into the open water of this narrow lane.

Battling the ice.

being at the ship's rail and was simply in the way.[25] A number of my shipmates walked or ran by, but none were very social or comradely. A great part of the confusion is undoubtedly due to the row the dogs were making, which prevents anyone from being able to concentrate on his job. Was rotating my ears in disgust at their rude noise when I was almost squashed by Crean's boots. 'Chippy! I'm sorry!' he exclaimed as I meowed indignantly. Everything is in confusion and Ship Order is lost. 'You all right, Mrs Chips?' he asked, picking me up and taking me to the port rail. 'Keep an eye on things from up here, if I were you,' he said. Assumed the station assigned by our Second Officer: being a member of an Expedition means often having to take on unexpected duties at a moment's notice. Watched as my mate led all hands over the side of the ship with saws and axes to chop up the ice.[26] Observed closely from my rail as a block of ice shot into the air from under the ship, overturning Crean. Groaning, he picked himself up from the ice and looked up to observe me closely observing him. Continued to supervise my shipmates until the Boss summoned everyone into the wardroom for a hot drink and told us we would just have to wait patiently until the winds or a current open the

[25]George Marston was a painter and the Expedition's artist. It is difficult to see how his official duties should have given him access to Mrs Chippy's station.
[26]In a desperate – and futile – attempt to cut the *Endurance* free from the ice.

ice again. The confusion today was completely unnecessary, and comes of certain persons allowing themselves to get carried away with excitement, not watching where they were going and interfering with other persons' jobs. I should imagine the Boss is quite disgusted. Determined the most constructive thing was to lead by example and prepared to sleep the hours patiently away, as the Boss instructed.[27]

January 29th. Awoke to find that the boiler fires have been shut down sometime over the past few days, which is a great shame as I enjoyed going

[27]As mentioned before, Mrs Chippy characteristically does not dwell on the same details which excite or frighten the rest of the crew, and the uninformed reader can be forgiven for admitting to a certain amount of unclarity concerning the events just related. Briefly, a northeasterly wind, sometimes at gale force, had blown continuously from 16 to 24 January, driving and compressing the loose pack ice against the Antarctic Continent, and with it the *Endurance*, which was now helplessly trapped. The Journal's silence on the events of this period indicate that Mrs Chippy's attention was employed on other matters, belowdecks, out of the wind. By contrast, the journals of Mrs Chippy's shipmates indicate their deep frustration at being paralysed only miles short of their destination, and the depth of their concern and fears that the ship might be trapped for a very long time – a fact that accounts for the haste and confused energy expended by them when an opportunity to cut their ship free from the ice was presented. Readers interested in exploring the 'inner lives' of the other Expedition members are invited to turn to these other accounts. They may conceivably obtain a 'clearer' picture of the exact events and circumstances and the emotions they inspired from these other sources, but will find none of Mrs Chippy's descriptive vividness.

down to visit the stokers and that little place they have on top of the old rags, close to the furnace. Outside, a rather dull day, the sky mouse-grey, the sea like frozen milk. From the watch rail, observed the sledging parties in the distance looking for seals on the ice, which means a return to proper routine. And where are the 'sledging' dogs? one might wish to know. Not on the ice and not pulling sledges, you may be sure, but lounging around in their kennels, making a lot of noise. Still, 'an idle dog lies low, until absolutely made to go' etc.[28] Returned to galley a little before teatime, in case Blackborow was running ahead of schedule.[29]

January 30th. My shipmates occupied today in a rousing game of football on the ice, all very merry and noisy and entertaining. Some of them play quite well, although perhaps not as well as they seem to think, no one being able to scoop the ball up on the run, which is a real art, very rarely properly done. In fact I used to play with my mate's daughter and was considered exceptionally skillful, going at full gallop across the grass and pouncing on the ball without ever breaking my stride, something I noticed none of my shipmates were quite able to do. Their game

---

[28]The source of this quotation has not been determined.
[29]Shackleton had been unwilling to trust the dogs to the ice, which as he noted was 'in a treacherous condition' – an eloquent indication of the limits of his faith in the intelligence of these foolish animals.

Mrs Chippy's shipmates enjoy a game of football.

ended and everyone came jogging up the gangway, sweating and laughing and red in the face. Later that evening we had a little singsong in the wardroom. I was feeling strangely restless until I came upon a piece of the chess set that Hurley and Hussey had been playing with earlier. I touched it very tentatively and found it rolled beautifully. I touched it a little harder and then chased after it as it rolled away, and soon I had an excellent rhythm going. My shipmates were quite astounded, and all stopped what they were doing to watch me as I spun around the floor; then they began to laugh and cheer, and Cheetham tried to intercept the chess piece but I outmanoeuvred him. 'Where were you when we needed you this afternoon, Mrs Chips?' asked the Skipper. I was suddenly very tired, but in a satisfying sort of way, and I went over to join my mate. 'Aye, Chippy's a champion,' he said, and pulled me onto his lap. A most agreeable day.

February 2nd. A busy day. Seven seals acquired for the ship's larder and a great deal of my time was spent seeing that they were properly stowed away. From my watch rail I observed as they were dragged to the ship, all brown and blood-soaked against the clean ice. As the sledgers drew closer to the ship, I raced ahead to greet them and to help get everything on board. It is a great shame that things do not smell so keenly in the cold. I could catch only a whiff or so, but in proper circumstances they must smell like enormous, freshly crunched mice. 'Heave ho, Chippy!' Frank Wild[30] called to me from the ice, above the usual rude barking of the dogs. 'Don't eat them all at once, now.' The slabs of butchered meat were handed up to the crew, and I escorted Cookie to the galley. After dinner, Sir Ernest discussed the necessity of consuming fresh meat to prevent scurvy. 'Do you suppose that's why Chippy does so well?' Worsley asked. 'All those fresh, raw mice?' 'Well, at least we know what we can do if we run short of seal,' said Hussey. 'Chippy can keep us provisioned.' Of course I would expect to do what I could for the common cause, but this ship is not so well stocked with mice as everyone might think. It is quite difficult to obtain what I do, and I'm not so sure there would be enough for everyone. Inevitably someone would have to go without. Such as Lees, for example.[31]

February 5th. Watch duties cancelled on account of blustery weather. I was taking advantage of this unexpected opportunity to catch up on a little sleep in the wardroom, when I was suddenly jolted awake

[30]Shackleton's trusted second-in-command, and the loyal companion of his earlier 1907–1909 expedition.
[31]Shackleton is credited with keeping a watchful eye over the health of his crew, and he was one of the first explorers to make a study of ways in which the bane of scurvy could be prevented. It becomes clear from this exchange, however, that Mrs Chippy was at least as foresighted as he in appreciating the antiscorbutic qualities of fresh meat.

at exactly the moment in my dream when I was leaning forward to look down into that squirrel hole at the bottom of the garden. Woke to find my shipmates crowding out the door. A moment later Wordie returned for his spectacles, which he had left on the table. 'Nasty,' he said to Cookie, who had come in from the galley. Both left looking very grave.[32]

Looked around and determined that I should probably stay and supervise things where I was, i.e., on my chair. Our ship runs very well. Everyone knows his job and once that little misunderstanding about the exact nature of my own duties and position, etc., was clarified things have gone very smoothly. Old Lees's idea that I should somehow restrict myself to my mate's cabin was completely impractical, as my job entails having access to all parts of the ship. I didn't make a fuss at the time, but just kept resolutely to my own routine, entering wardroom, galley, cabins, fo'c'sle, hold, bunks and so forth as the need arose. Everything soon settled down and now whenever I enter any room I am greeted warmly by my shipmates, who also willingly share a little something from their

[32]The winds of a northeasterly gale had worked upon the pack, causing the ice to jostle against the ship – a hint of its deadly potential. The Journal presents numerous such examples of Mrs Chippy's unruffled composure in the face of danger.

breakfast, lunch or dinner bowls. Resumed my little snooze and was woken by my shipmates coming in for their tea, all covered with snow. Everyone seemed somewhat snappy and antisocial, so I left to help Blackborow in the galley. 'Chippy, we lost our chance,' said my mate, as we went to bed. 'The ice opened and if the Boss had had our steam up, we could have reeved her through.' My mate knows a great deal about such nautical matters and so forth, and often tells me what my shipmates are doing wrong. As his mate, I take these confidences very seriously. To sleep between his ankles.[33]

February 10th. My shipmates all very pleased to see me again, Sir Ernest in particular commenting on how nice it was to have me back. I rejoined everyone at teatime in the wardroom, stretching my legs as I came forward and nonchalantly resuming my old place. 'It's Chippy!' everyone cried, scraping back their chairs to greet me. 'Chippy's here! Mrs Chippy's back!' Was greeted very warmly, and Blackborow came out with my bowl from the galley, properly filled with my teatime milk. 'We thought you'd been blown overboard, Mrs Chips,'

[33]Mrs Chippy's mate was a much-experienced shipwright, unafraid of anyone and known for speaking his mind – qualities for which lesser men feared him. Even Shackleton had written that McNeish was 'the only man I am not dead certain of . . . he is a very good workman but of a dour disposition' (letter to Ernest Perris, 30 November 1914).

he said, stroking me. 'We looked everywhere.' 'Now, quite seriously, where on earth do you think Chippy's been?' asked Crean, as I strolled around the tables after I'd finished my milk, greeting my shipmates one by one. 'We searched every blasted corner of the ship.' 'The hold,' said Cheetham, 'Chippy must have got locked in the hold again,' which is all a lot of nonsense. 'I went through the hold with a fine-tooth comb,' said Blackborow, 'and I'll take my oath Chippy wasn't there.' 'I'm placing my money on one of the cupboards,' said Worsley. 'Or the lab. Did anyone check the lab? Or Hurley's darkroom?' Supplemented my tea with sardines and butter, etc., then took a little snooze while my shipmates continued their discussion of the geography and interior design of our ship. Seal liver in my bowl for dinner. Bunked with my mate. 'I wasn't concerning myself with your whereabouts, Mrs Chips,' said my mate in his growly voice as we went to bed, 'having been through that particular little routine enough times to know better.' Things are more peaceful now that everyone has stopped stomping around in their boots, calling and yelling and banging my bowl and moving furniture etc. etc.[34] A very pleasant day.

[34]Evidently, the search for Mrs Chippy had been quite thorough. The journals of Mrs Chippy's shipmates indicate that these so-called missing days had been cold and uneventful, and that Mrs Chippy was completely justified in taking a little time out.

February 11th. Bright sun, but very cold. Engines all rumbling. On deck early for my watch, coinciding with noon sunshine. Briefly joined the Boss and Skipper on the bridge and the three of us discussed our circumstances.[35] In the afternoon, the Boss summoned the entire ship's company aft by the wheel. 'See what you can do,' he called out to us. 'One, two, ready – go!' Immediately all my shipmates began jumping up and down and running from side to side. Ears back, whiskers forward, I observed them carefully, then bounded out to join them. My shipmates cheered me loudly as I raced from side to side with them, until the ship suddenly lurched beneath our paws and the Boss sang out, 'You've done it, boys! She's free!' The dogs were barking like mad of course, having no idea about the purpose of our nautical operations. I suspect they are bewildered much of the time by what goes on around them. The Boss told Lees to bring his little motor sledge out for a trial run on the ice, where it sputtered around to the great amusement of the sailors, while Lees kept saying that the ice was 'too bumpy.' Later, I overheard the Boss telling Wild that 'it looks like we'll be using dogs after all,' and that 'if the dogs are as keen to pull sledges as they are to fight, all will be well.' I am afraid this is unduly optimistic.

---

[35]The *Endurance* was not only frozen into the ice pack, but had become jammed against a floe. The events that follow were efforts to shake the ship free.

February 12th. Still stuck fast. On deck in readiness in the event that we might all try and shake the ship free again, but evidently it's a different kind of stuckness than yesterday. My shipmates occupied with a thorough washing of the decks, entailing moving and sousing the kennels with very comical results. Things became a little too confused and unpredictable, however, with the dogs running rather too freely, and I decided to return to the wardroom and await my tea.[36] Am trying out a very nice place in the Skipper's cabin.

February 14th. Ship routine disrupted and everyone on the ice all yesterday chopping away with their picks and shovels.[37] Breakfast cold, lunch and dinner late. Assumed watch post at bow, and observing that my shipmates were working quite some distance from the ship, decided to

[36]In later entries, Mrs Chippy refers to taking tea in the *galley*, an apparent inconsistency that has confused many scholars. Most probably, Mrs Chippy regularly enjoyed two teas – one in the galley prepared by Blackborow (usually warm milk) and a second in the wardroom with other members of the ship's company (sardines on toast, butter, hot drinks of Bovril, etc.). Similarly, Mrs Chippy had access to two dinner shifts, one for the forward hands and a second for the wardroom. The Journal's striking record of intimate details of ship life is one of its chief virtues.

[37]Mrs Chippy's shipmates were trying to take advantage of lanes of open water that had appeared in the ice ahead of the *Endurance*, so as to cut a path to freedom. They had been hard at work since early morning.

stroll over to see how the dogs were getting on whilst their 'minders' were so occupied. Made my way across the kennel roofs, stationing myself above 'Captain' and opposite 'Snapper' or 'Skipper' or 'Simper' or whatever foolish name he calls himself, focusing intently on the tip of his wet shining nose. What a lot of noise! These dogs become quite lost in the cloud of their own barking.[38] Continued to study him and his companions, noting in particular their uncouth frosty mouths and runny noses. I must say, it is a great shame the public dog washings have been discontinued since we ran into this colder weather, they were so very comical and entertaining. Neatly cleaned my own paws and whiskers, then stretched and made my way back towards the hatch, while the dogs lunged and snarled at the ends of their stout chains. My Watch completed, decided my energy would be best employed below, and went to check on critical areas. Conducted an investigation of my shipmates' bunks and cabins in their absence, determining that Crean's cabin has a place worth trying out sometime in the future. Bowl still empty in galley. Determined to wait by galley stove for

[38]This evocative, almost lyrical line beautifully captures the image of the dogs wreathed in the 'smoke' of their own breath as it vaporizes in the cold air. Surviving cinematographic film taken by photographer Frank Hurley shows the aptness of Mrs Chippy's observation: a striking image shows one of these animals with plumes of 'smoke' billowing from his grinning mouth.

*Mrs Chippy's shipmates attempt to cut a path for
the* Endurance.

Blackborow to turn up and attend to his job. Inexplicably, I must have dozed off, for I was awoken some hours later by my shipmates hurrying in, stamping their feet and clapping their cold, red hands – I must have been more worn out than I had realized.[39] Dinner at last, but very hastily prepared. This disruption of ship routine is very bad for Ship Morale.

February 15th. Rudely jolted awake by rumbling and banging and lurching of our ship. Breakfast unsatisfactory, being rather sloppily prepared and the banging and bumping of our ship making it very unpleasant for me to eat.[40] Returned to my place at the head of Bakewell's bed to weather the disturbance. Up again shortly before noon, just as my shipmates were returning from the ice, stumping downstairs looking very wet and disconsolate. The Boss gathered us all in the wardroom for lunch and hot drinks, and gave a little

---

[39]Mrs Chippy's shipmates worked on the ice until close to midnight, having succeeded in chopping out a 150-yard-long channel towards the open lane of water that lay so tantalizingly near.

[40]Mrs Chippy's shipmates had resumed their work on the channel in the ice early that morning. When they had advanced the channel as far as their strength enabled them, Captain Worsley gunned the ship's engines and tried repeatedly to ram the *Endurance* through the remaining four hundred or so yards of ice that lay between them and the open lane of water. It was the ship's repeated pounding of the ice that was so disruptive to Mrs Chippy's breakfast routine.

speech. 'It can't be helped, boys,' he said, looking around at everyone slumped over in their chairs. 'After so much work, you deserved success, but we can't fight Nature. We'll have to wait it out.' My shipmates all started murmuring about the ice while they had their lunch. 'Eighteen feet thick if it's an inch,' said my mate. 'There's no tool known to Man that can carve that lot up.' Took a little snooze until teatime, waking to find my shipmates still very disconsolate and grumbly. Wandered around under the table, coming out beside Lees, who was sitting in my chair, pretending to read. Sociably indicated that I would join him on his book and was rudely rebuffed. 'Easy!' said Worsley to him, while all my shipmates stopped what they were doing to watch. 'No need to fly off like that!' 'I'm trying to read,' said Lees, going all pink and puffy. 'I suppose that's still allowed, is it?' 'Knock it off,' said Cheetham. 'Chippy was only trying to sit down.' 'Oh, and I suppose Mrs Chippy now ranks higher than I do?' said Lees in his whiny, sarcastic voice. My mate put his big tea mug down, and looked at Lees. 'Chippy is less bloody useless,' he said, in his growly voice, 'and wasn't skulking in the wheelhouse avoiding work like some blaggards I know.' Lees got very pink, while all my shipmates laughed and I wound my way around my mate's big boots. Joined my mate and then Cheetham on their laps for some comradely socializing. Awoke at dinner-time to find everyone still morose and out of humour, but cheerier in the evening, when we held one of our gramophone-playing sessions. 'We have to roll with the swell, Mrs Chips,' said my mate as we turned in. 'It may be we'll be wintering here. It's only God's will that will see us out before spring.' I believe in taking one thing at a time, the most important concern at the moment being the restoration of Ship Routine.

February 18th. Up early around noon to find my shipmates very restless, going in and out all day long, and letting in cold air and snow. Visited my friends in the fo'c'sle, where they were discussing our winter plans. 'Well, I don't much fancy sitting here for the next six months,' said Stevenson. 'We should have anchored in one of those bays we passed back there on the glacier.' 'What are we going to do all winter?' asked Holness. 'It's going to be pitchy black.'[41] 'That won't make no difference,' said McLeod. 'Seeing as it's going to be pitchy here, or there, or wherever you might choose to anchor.' 'Yes, but we'd have been on land,' grumbled Stevenson, 'or close to it. And at a place with a name, not stuck in the middle of who knows where.' 'Chippy doesn't mind about the dark, do you, Chippy?' said Bakewell. 'Chip-

[41]The day before, on 17 February, the sun had set at midnight, denoting the end of summer and the advent of the dark night of Polar winter – an event noted with regret by Mrs Chippy's shipmates in their own diaries. By contrast, there is ample evidence in the Journal that Mrs Chippy was undismayed by the dark.

py's the only one who's come properly equipped,' said McLeod.[42] 'Good thick coat; good vision in the Polar darkness.' My shipmates stopped their grumbling and turned their attention to me properly, suddenly becoming very cheery. 'Strong sense of curiosity,' said Blackborow. 'Very necessary for an explorer.' My shipmates were now all very merry and amused. 'And what about footwear?' said Bakewell. 'All that Finnesko the Boss is so proud of isn't a patch on what Chippy's wearing.'[43] Enjoyed my visit with my shipmates until tea-time, when I accompanied Blackborow over his shoulder to the galley. I thought about this conversation as I went to bed. It is true that I seem to have weathered the rigours of the Expedition better than most of my shipmates. I never complain about the cold like they do, for instance, nor ever grumble about my duties. Certain characteristics necessary to this job cannot be acquired. One doesn't just 'decide' to become an Explorer.

February 20th. A most unfortunate development. Cookie twisted his knee playing football and Lees has been appointed as his replacement, which could jeopardize the success of the entire Expedition. He

[42]William Stevenson and Ernest Holness were both trawler hands from Hull, who served as firemen, or stokers, on the *Endurance*. Thomas McLeod was an able seaman.
[43]Shackleton was indeed pleased with the 'Finnesko' outer boots he had acquired for his Expedition members. Made of reindeer hide, with furry uppers and bare skin pads, they were sometimes fitted with crampons for traction.

already tried to send me out of the galley when I was taking my accustomed place by the stove, which is quite outrageous and a clear breach of Ship Rules pertaining to the execution of jobs and duties by other persons. Fortunately, Blackborow remains on galley duty and so was on hand to set him straight. 'Mrs Chippy stays in here,' said Blackborow very firmly. 'Cookie has Chippy on permanent mouse detail.' 'Are there mice, then?' said stupid Lees, looking around. 'Not with Chippy here,' said Blackborow. I looked levelly, with un-blinking eyes, at Lees. I don't think I would be making quite so much noise if  my motor sledges didn't work. 'Well, I suppose Chippy stays,' he said at last. Blackborow made a loud, clattering noise in the sink, and Lees went over to watch him, while I took my place beside the stove. Tea and dinner served on time and my bowl properly prepared, but it will be important to remain vigilant.[44]

February 21st. Samson and Hackenschmidt in a terrific fight over their breakfast, very noisy and

[44]Lees as it turned out knew very little about cooking, despite the boasting that had won him this interim appointment. To his diary he confided that 'Blackborow – our excellent stowaway who is now acting as pantry boy . . . is really a most excellent . . . young fellow. I soon find that he knows quite a lot about cooking & I confide in him that I know nothing & that I rely upon him to pull me through' (T. H. Orde-Lees, diary, 19 February 1915). Lees, therefore, jolly well had to toe the line with Mrs Chippy's friend while in the galley.

exciting. These dogs of ours sit all day with their eyes on the main hatch, waiting expectantly for the first appearance of their minders coming up with the biscuit box, then fall all over each other in greedy excitement when they see them. My own breakfast of chopped seal liver waiting for me in my bowl, eaten quietly in the privacy of the galley.

February 22nd. Seal for breakfast, lunch and dinner. Milk and butter from plates for tea, during which time the Boss called for attention and made an announcement. 'Well, men,' he said, 'it seems we'll be wintering here.' My shipmates all started murmuring and mumbling, until Frank Wild gave them a look that said be quiet. 'If I had guessed a month ago we'd be so caught,' the Boss continued, 'I would have established a winter base at one of the landing bays of the great glacier.' He paused. 'Many of you must have been wondering why I did not.' Everyone started looking down at the table and fiddling with their mugs and plates. 'My mistake,' said the Boss. 'I wanted to begin the land march as Far South as we could manage. My mistake,' he said again. 'We all have faith in your judgement, Boss,' said Frank Wild suddenly, and all my shipmates cheered and banged the table, while I rubbed along their boots in approval of these hearty words. In fact I am in complete agreement with the Boss about staying here, as nothing has been gained by disrupting ship routine and wearing ourselves out in the cold and so forth, and besides our Ship is very cosy where it is. Respectfully wound my way against the Boss's boots to show my complete support. 'Thank you, men,' he said, looking very cheered. 'Thank you, Mrs Chippy,' he said, bending to greet me with a head rub, while all my shipmates laughed very cheerily. Sir Ernest and I understand each other perfectly. Back at the docks in London, it was Sir Ernest who greeted me as I accompanied my mate up the gangplank, on his shoulder, saying, 'Well then, Chips, who's this you've brought along? This must be *Mrs* Chippy!' My mate had earlier had some doubts about having me ship with him, so Sir Ernest must have been relieved to see that I was coming after all.[45]

February 24th. Up early to ensure that my break-fast bowl was properly prepared, as indeed it was. Strolled into the wardroom, where the Boss was announcing certain changes in our routine, N.B.,

---

[45]Of this day, which marked the relinquishment of his dreams, Shackleton wrote: 'The summer had gone; indeed the summer had scarcely been with us at all . . . I could not doubt that the *Endurance* was confined for the winter. Gentle breezes from the east, south, and south-west did not disturb the hardening floe. The seals were disappearing and the birds were leaving us. The land showed still in fair weather on the distant horizon, but it was beyond our reach now, and regrets for havens that lay behind us were vain. We must wait for the spring, which may bring us better fortune' (Shackleton, *South*, p. 35). Although unremarked by Mrs Chippy, this day also represents the Furthest South attained by the *Endurance*, touching the 77th parallel. From this point on, the stricken ship began its long, helpless northward drift within the pack ice.

from now on only one watch will be on duty at night, which greatly pleases my shipmates.[46] No mention was made of my own night duties, i.e., mouse patrol in the various storage areas, investigating passageways, etc., so I imagine they will remain unaffected. The Boss also ordered the afterhold to be cleared and a complete inventory of stores taken, very necessary to weathering the winter. Peggy Lees has been made 'storekeeper' to the great amusement of my shipmates, and has been bustling around very self-importantly with his little notebook.[47] 'Please, Peggy, can I have another biscuit?' asked Cheetham. '*Exactly* how many biscuits are left?' asked Macklin, while Lees went all pink and puffy. During teatime, I made a little detour down to the hold, just to see how things had been arranged and so forth, and to do a little inventory taking of my own just in case Lees got it all wrong. I know the important tins by sight, of course, and was able to establish that we are well supplied with all the staples, i.e., powdered and Nestlé's condensed milk, sardines, tinned rabbit and Bovril. Some of the

[46]With the cessation of regular sailors' watches, the *Endurance* officially became a winter station, as opposed to an active ship, an eloquent indication that any and all hope of getting free of the ice that winter had been abandoned.

[47]A 'Peggy' in ship parlance was the person responsible for certain domestic fetch and carrying. In the case of Thomas Orde-Lees, the nickname – one of many he was given – was also a disparaging reference to his fussy, 'old-womanish' ways, of which Mrs Chippy's mate McNeish was particularly contemptuous.

other things will have to be used more carefully, but that should be all right. I look forward to this next stage of our Expedition.

February 26th. A splendid few days. The Boss wisely ordered the removal of the dogs from our ship and they are now housed in little kennels along the floe beside us. I just happened to be on deck during their forced disembarkation and so was able to observe the entire proceedings. What a lot of noise! My word, these dogs were very reluctant to go overboard! Observed closely as each one was dragged off the ship and much hysterical baying and barking. Crean looked up from the ice and saw me sitting on my watch rail with my ears well back on account of the noise. He laughed and called up to me, 'Disgusting racket, isn't it, Chippy?' I arched my back in agreement, and leaned over the rail for a better look. Pushing and fighting and barking and baying, they were led to their little dogloos, which have been built in a line across the ice floe, and which look very snug; not as snug as the ship to be sure, but quite adequate to their needs. A length of wire stretches from one end of the line to the other, and to this each dog is securely tethered in a manner that allows him room to run, although not to run too far.[48] It is an excellent

[48]The word *dogloo* was apparently coined by Worsley, but readily adopted by Mrs Chippy. The careful description of the layout of these ice kennels indicates that Mrs Chippy had observed their construction with particular attention and interest.

*The dogs are led onto the ice; Mrs Chippy is
watching out of frame.*

arrangement. The ship is now free and clear and the dogs can start their winter conditioning; if they are going to be pulling sledges over snow and ice, it is in their own best interest to become acclimatized to these particular elements as soon as possible.

February 27th. Up early to observe dogs harnessed and fitted to their sledges. I must say, these dogs of ours are very energetic! Dancing and prancing around, they all ran off in one direction, pulling their little sledges; then all turned around and ran back again. And for this they have come all the way to Antarctica! Observed their foolish manoeuvres until my interest began to flag, then went below to finish up my watch. Helped my shipmates with the new warm clothing they were issued, going over everything very carefully and overseeing where it was stored. Joined Blackborow in the galley, where Lees was pretending to prepare our luncheon; in fact he doesn't know what he's doing, but only copies Blackborow. Refreshed myself with a little snooze by the galley stove and strolled on deck again in time to join the Boss and Skipper as they observed the dogs finishing up their exercises, all panting and exhausted. 'Well, they seem eager enough,' said the Boss, 'but they've got some work to do.' Sir Ernest is most perceptive. Like him I am only interested in the success and welfare of the Expedition and my interest in the dogs is purely professional. A very pleasant day.

The 'sledging' dogs are prepared for their exercise.
Photo taken from Mrs Chippy's rail.

March 1st. Blizzard. My shipmates all inside, complaining about the cold and having nothing to do etc. etc. In fact I am always occupied and if one looks around carefully these are always plenty of places to be warm. Nonetheless, the Boss addressed the ship's company today, saying we would soon be making winter arrangements. Everyone very restless and at a loose end, with Hurley and Wild talking incessantly about the construction of the new dogloos, regaling us all with details of how they selected the ice slabs to build them, how they cut the ice slabs, how they raised the ice slabs, how they assembled the ice slabs and on and on, boring everyone around them – Hurley is one of those persons who needs to feel himself the centre of attention, and likes to imagine that everything he does is of great importance.[49] Left the wardroom early to join my mate in bed. 'Minus two degrees,' he said in his growly voice, looking at his thermometer. 'Snuggle up, Mrs Chips. This cabin's not fit for man nor beast.' Bunked with my mate between his ankles, relocating to his chest in the middle of the night.

March 2nd. Blizzard. Joined my mate and the Boss in the hold where we discussed the refitting of this area for winter arrangements. Walked the area with my mate, looking things over with him, and

[49]Hurley's nickname was 'The Prince.'

also as it happened discovering a nest of mice that had been disturbed by the winter arrangements. Pursued my own duties while my mate continued his, obtaining two specimens, one of them quite exceptional in terms of both tail length and overall weight. My mate being still occupied, decided to share my catch with Blackborow, who was in the galley peeling potatoes and chatting with Bakewell.

'There now, just what you wanted,' said Bakewell to Blackborow, while I showed them my mouse, doing a few basic manoeuvres with it and so forth to remind them of  how it's done. Blackborow was just bending down to retrieve it when old Lees came in. 'Oh no!' he exclaimed. 'It's a mouse,' he said, stopping at the doorway. 'Chippy caught it just as it was heading for the biscuit tin,' said Bakewell, very coolly. 'Oh,' said Lees, and watched carefully while I gave him a little demonstration of how a mouse works, tossing and rolling it etc. very adroitly. 'Lucky thing Mrs Chippy's here,' said Blackborow brightly, picking up my mouse by its tail and moving towards the stove. There was a pause. 'I hadn't realized quite how things stood,' said Lees at last, sheepishly. 'Well done, Mrs Chippy,' he said, and gave me an awkward pat, not a proper stroke or head rub. Lees knows nothing about mice, and wouldn't know what to do with one if it sat in his bowl. Bakewell left with a big wink, while Lees began to fuss around getting things ready for tea and Blackborow prepared my teatime milk. 'I wouldn't push it, Mrs Chips,' he said as he bent down to present me with my bowl. 'From now on I'd confine the mousing to the hold.' A most engaging day.

March 3rd. Blizzard lifted and my watch resumed. Immediately made my way through the drifts of snow to my watch rail so as to observe the dogs confined in their dogloos, covering their wet noses with their bushy tails. Closely observed my shipmates dig out the entrances to the dogloos and the dogs come out to shake the snow from their fur. Walked along the gunwales, stretching my legs, as they were a bit tight after having slept so deeply curled up by the galley stove. Ignored the raucous barking of dogs and returned belowdecks to see to the establishment of winter arrangements for the Ship's officers and Scientists in the hold, where we will all be much warmer. My mate is in charge of the whole proceedings, of course, and he and I went down to the 'tween deck to look things over while all other hands cleared everything out. My mate and I enjoy all aspects of ship life, but we both look forward to the opportunity of exercising our professional skills.

March 4th. Up early with my mate to begin construction of the new quarters. He and I have worked together in the shipyards and in his work-shop at home, so I am very familiar with this line of work. It is exceedingly gratifying to be able to show my shipmates my expertise in this regard, as up until now they have known me only as a Sailor. My mate selected his tools and I checked each one carefully, inspecting it minutely and testing it with the tip of my paw. Then while he cut and sawed, I raced around the bare floorboards, catching loose objects and bowling them along towards him. I also helped him by rubbing against the planks of wood as he stood them upright to make walls, showing him if they were stable or not. Frank Hurley fancies himself as an amateur carpenter and so was inter-ested to watch us work. 'Do you think it would be easier if Chippy went on top?' he ventured at one point, as I was catching the long wood shavings that dangled and fell off the planks of wood. This was nonsense. There were dozens of hands to do the work up top, so I doubt I could have made it much 'easier' for them, whereas I was the only one who could help my mate. 'Chippy's all right here,' said my mate in his growly voice. He and I have a very good working relationship. Before he left home to join our ship, he debated with his family whether I should accompany him. But I came upon his duffel bag and tools all packed and ready to go in the front hall and inspected them very carefully. And when he came to collect them, he found me sleeping on his toolbox. 'Chippy's coming with me,' he said to his wife. Although I am very fond of his family, it's he who is my mate.

March 6th. Cookie is back!! The men gave him a big cheer at the breakfast table. Lees had rationed meals, serving biscuits instead of bread and he was always watching to see what Blackborow put in my bowl. I thought this very bad for Ship Morale. Joined my shipmates in a little singsong in the evening.

March 8th. Worked with my mate in the Boss's cabin, which is full of an interesting array of items – piles of jerseys, a typewriter with clicking keys, shelves of books, maps and charts and so forth – all of which bear a thorough investigation, although every time I attempted to go up to examine them my mate indicated that he needed me with him at ground level.[50] After he had finished and we had left, I returned to the cabin on my own, as there were a few things I felt I should look over to my satisfaction, so as to finish the job properly. I was just standing on the desk looking at the bed when Crean passed by. 'I don't think that's what you want to do,' he said out of the blue, and escorted me under his arm to the galley where Blackborow was making a stew. 'Your friend here was about to settle in the Boss's bed,' Crean said. I looked at

[50]Shackleton alone of the wardroom did not take up new winter quarters. Instead Mrs Chippy and McNeish 'winterized' his cabin with insulation. The new quarters constructed by the carpenter and his mate were for the officers and scientists, with Wild, Worsley, Crean and Marston moving to cubicles established within the old wardroom. Mrs Chippy's friends in the fo'c'sle stayed in their quarters, which were sufficiently warm.

Chippy and his mate.

Blackborow and mewed; I wasn't interested in taking over his bed, I was just looking things over, which is part of my job! Blackborow gave me a piece of seal from the stew. 'Some people are funny that way, Chippy,' he said, stroking me. 'Some people don't like having their beds walked all over with your big wet snowy paws.' He leaned over to whisper to me: 'Besides, the Boss can't let himself be too familiar. Think of his dignity!'

March 13th. The winter arrangements are splendid, and very conducive to proper rest. 'Good evening, Mrs Chippy, enjoying your little four-day snooze?' asked Crean, who was passing through and watching everyone settle in. We sailors are a rough lot and banter of this kind is entirely common amongst us. In fact Crean is keenly aware that I have been completely absorbed over the past few days working in the cubicles, assessing their particular character and differences, and respective distances from the stove.[51] 'Excuse me, Mrs Chippy, but I

[51]Scholars have long noted discrepancies in the accounts given by Mrs Chippy's shipmates of the winter relocation. McNeish, for example, says very specifically that 'all hands migrated this evening . . . turned in my new cabin' on Saturday, 13 March. Shackleton, however, implies that the Expedition members 'took possession of the cubicles that had been built' on Wednesday, 10 March (Shackleton, *South*, p. 40). Mrs Chippy's Journal clarifies this apparent contradiction. Shackleton was undoubtedly refer-ring to Mrs Chippy's occupation of the new quarters some days ahead of the other Expedition members.

*Bobby Clark and James Wordie were often visited
by Mrs Chippy in their cubicle in the Ritz.*

think I've been assigned this bunk,' said Hussey, coming into the cubicle I happened to be occupying, with his big bundles. 'I thought Chippy had claimed the cubicle next door,' said Crean, who was leaning around the partition, 'and the one next door to that; and the one across the way.' In fact I haven't 'claimed' anything in particular. My official berth is with my mate and Mr Cheetham, but of course I will be trying other places on occasion, especially as our new accommodations are so close and sociable.[52] Helped my shipmates sort out all their bundles and blankets, examining each article minutely as it was unpacked. Continued my investigations while my shipmates had their dinner. 'I've watched Chippy systematically go through every last object that's been brought in here,' said Crean, as everyone turned in their chairs to watch me finish my patrol. 'The First Mate's on the job,' said the Boss, smiling. Sir Ernest knows that he can absolutely count on me to be scrupulous in the fulfillment of my duties. Continued my investigations well into the night, visiting nearly every bunk long after my shipmates had gone to bed, and even after many of them begged me to relax my duties and go to sleep.

[52]The new between-deck quarters, nicknamed 'the Ritz,' were made up of six cubicles opening onto a common area in which meals were served, and which was filled by a long table and the stove originally intended for the hut that Shackleton had planned to build as a land base on the Antarctic continent. In sailorly custom, the cubicles were given distinctive names by their inhabitants, such as 'The Billabong,' 'The Anchorage,' 'The Fumarole.' Mrs Chippy occupied 'The Sailor's Rest.'

Mrs Chippy's berth.

March 15th. ⋆N.B. Winter Routine Begins To-day⋆ Observed Wild enter Sir Ernest's cabin today after lunch, and decided to clean my paws and whiskers in the passage outside and so happened to overhear the Boss say that next to the ice, the crew's greatest enemy over the winter will be 'tedium.' It is true that while my own days are filled with activity, I have noted that many of my shipmates are at a loose end for things to do. My mate says that Lees 'hasn't done a stroke of work since leaving London,' for example. I myself am very self-disciplined by nature and have set myself a strict winter regime: Wake at 2:00 P.M.; stretch, wash, take breakfast by the galley stove, greet shipmates etc. On deck for Watch shortly after 3:00. At this time I also take my exercise, sharpening my claws on the mast, practising manoeuvres amid the coils of rope and so forth. Often I help my shipmates in shipping seal meat and blubber, or keeping an eye on the dogs below. I finish my watch just before four, and return to the galley for my teatime milk – if Blackborow is in charge, he sometimes heats it for me. After this I may snooze by the stove or help my shipmates with their various desk jobs. Many have notes and Journals to write up at this time and I help keep the pages of their notebooks flat by sitting on them while they work. Also Blackborow has his books to attend to, as the Boss has told him he must keep up his schooling, and naturally I help him with these. This is also the time I compose my own mental notes of the day's events for my Log. This time is very social, and I'm often summoned from one end of the big table to the other by persons needing my assistance. 'Hoy! – Mrs Chippy – what's this down here?' Crean called the other day. I went to investigate and found the bowl of a broken pipe rolling around the floor. Instantly I apprehended it, and my shipmates were greatly pleased. 'Chippy's keeping everything in order,' said Crean and everyone laughed their approval. After dinner with my shipmates at 6:00 P.M., I often join my mate for a brief constitutional evening stroll around the deck, taking in the night air and observing the icy dogloos below, and the dogs huddled around them. I usually have a saucer of milk before retiring for the night. Generally I bunk with my mate, or with Blackborow. Once everyone's asleep, I take the day's final, midnight watch, and carefully walk around my shipmates as they sleep, examining their possessions, just ensuring everything's in order. This is the time that I learn the most – for example, Lees saves and hides scraps of food to eat in secret away from everyone else, and has his own little nest of things hidden in the hold. The Boss is often awake when I pass his cabin; Marston usually lies awake when he's supposed to be sleeping, but when he's supposed to be on night duty, he sleeps on the job. It is also during this final watch that I do my best mousing. I know intimately all of our ship's storage areas and generally catch one good mouse a night, which serves as both vital physical and mental tonic. Before turning in for the night, I sometimes visit with the watchman, who is always pleased to see me, sharing cocoa and sardines and so forth. I return to my berth to finish the night with my shipmates. This winter routine has fallen very naturally into place.

March 17th. Slept somewhat later than usual, on account of snowy gale keeping us all indoors. My shipmates very restless and argumentative.[53] Joined my mate on his constitutional stroll at sunset. Sky the colour of seal's blood, snow on the decks glowing. The Boss was up top too and called to my mate, pointing to the horizon. My mate put his pipe in his mouth and held me up to the rail. 'What about that, Chippy?' he said. ' "The molten mirror of the skies." '

March 18th. Busy helping the Scientists, who have set up a special place to examine parts of penguins, rocks, ice, sea things, etc., all central to conducting an Expedition. Although not trained as a Scientist, I was able to help in this regard and made a number of I think important observations –

---

[53] According to McNeish's diary, the 'arguments' were about the war, which had just broken out as the *Endurance* left England. In a later entry, Mrs Chippy's mate remarks that the crew 'unanimously hope that the war God has been crushed without any further loss of life & . . . we all sincerely hope the Russians will capture him for if Briton do they will set him up in a palace for the ratepayers to keep' (H. McNeish, diary, 10 April 1915).

certainly as important as some of theirs, i.e., that there are different types of ice and some rocks are older than others. Discussed a Mr Darwin, who says that everyone eventually adapts to his surroundings. Only the fittest animals survive here, which is why there are purportedly no mice at all in Antarctica, as they would obviously be no match for the penguins, let alone the seals. This is the sort of information that distinguishes Explorers from lay-persons, and certainly it all makes one think. Studied the landscape very carefully on my constitutional watch. Everything is much bigger than one might imagine. Was absorbed in such philosophical speculations when the Skipper walked by. 'Why Chippy!' he said, 'you're still out. What are you thinking about, eh? That nice piece of seal you had for dinner?' Rudely disrupted from my speculations by the Skipper removing me from my rail and escorting me belowdecks under his arm. 'Your mate will be looking for you,' he said. Bunked with my mate between his ankles.

March 22nd. Occupied for most of the day with routine ship duties. Went forward to see how things were going in the fo'c'sle, joining Blackborow on his bunk, in the crook of his knee. Blackborow entertained us all with a little pantomime, demonstrating the correct manner in which to roll over, or change position when bunking with a shipmate who might be lying between one's ankles, or in the crook of one's knee, etc. 'Now,' said Blackborow, 'this is the

The Watchman's tale. Mrs Chippy is behind the feet of Chips McNeish (with pipe), out of view.

A mid-winter morning in the Ritz: Blackborow with a block of ice (to be melted for water) and Chips McNeish on left. Scientists on right.

tricky part. Hold your breath and keeping the engaged leg in place, carefully turn yourself over – ' 'I see,' said Wally How, laughing, as Blackborow lay face down in his pillow, his leg still crooked correctly. 'Now, does Chippy move at any stage of this operation?' 'Oh, no!' said Bakewell, very amused at this question. 'Chippy doesn't move a whisker. Chippy shouldn't even be aware you're turning.' This is a bit of an exaggeration, as of course I am 'aware' of such shifts and changes, but as long

as they are done with due attention and care I don't make a fuss about it. 'Slide the op- posing leg over,' Black- borow continued, from the pillow, 'until you encounter the First Mate's presence.' 'Which is unmistakable,' said How. 'Which is unmistakable,' Blackborow agreed. 'Carefully exchange your legs and the manoeuvre is complete. Of course you may pull a muscle or two here and there, and lose a bit of sleep, but that's another matter.' Blackborow is very droll and amusing, but I am glad he gave this little demonstration, which I think was instructive. It represents one of those very basic courtesies one assumes everyone has been brought up to know, and yet I have been rudely awoken in the middle of the night by persons who roll and toss them- selves regardless of the whereabouts of their fellow shipmate. To a great extent the success and morale of an Expedition depends upon attention to such niceties.

March 24th. A rather dull day. As the Boss had so clearly foreseen, a number of my shipmates don't have enough to do, and so pass their time monopolizing our dinner with their discussion and comparison of the various sledging teams, Wild and Hurley being especially culpable of this and apparently unmindful of the fact that not everyone in the room finds this an especially engrossing topic, certainly not what we want to hear at the end of a long day. In fact I have observed some of these 'remarkable' sledging sessions and they entail harnessing the dogs to empty sledges and then shouting nonsense words after them as they careen and veer across the ice.[54] Later, the dogs are unharnessed, separated from each other's throats, calmed, fed and almost shown to the very entrance of their dogloos. We are down to fifty something of them now, the rest having succumbed to worms and 'stomach ailments,' although how they managed to pick up worms here is anybody's guess. Yawned and stretched, then went over to one of the cubicles and began scratching my claws on the walls just to break the monotony of this

[54]Shackleton records that 'the orders used by the drivers were "Mush" (Go on), "Gee" (Right), "Haw" (Left), and "Whoa" (Stop),' a demeaning 'baby talk' to which the dogs were apparently receptive (Shackleton, *South*, p. 41).

tedious dinner conversation, and went on doing so after I was told to stop. Finally, my mate came over to get me and put me very securely on his lap. 'What's up with Mrs Chippy this evening?' asked the Skipper. I ignored him when he tried to stroke me and went to sleep with only a minimum of purr.

March 25th. Slept a little later than usual and had to cut short my deck watch. Decided to visit the fo'c'sle hands and found Bakewell, How, McCarthy, McLeod, Cookie and Blackborow all in their quarters.[55] 'Hello, Chippy!' said Bakewell, as he saw me curling around the doorway, and hoisted me onto his bed. I began to knead the blanket and looked around, purring. 'Tired of the comforts of the wardroom?' he asked, stroking me. I turned around a few times to settle my position properly, then lay down next to his knee. By a coincidence they were also discussing Mr Darwin, who McLeod says is wicked. McLeod won't eat penguins because they are the souls of dead sailors. He also says that gold has been found inside some penguins, which is probably why the scientists are always cutting them open. It was very pleasant to lie and listen to all this interesting discussion above my head, and to hear another point of view. I half rolled on my side and was

[55] Walter How, Timothy McCarthy and Thomas McLeod were all, like Bakewell, able seamen.

Bobby Clark working peacefully in his lab; note the array of intriguing jars and bottles.

later awoken by Blackborow. He and Cookie were going back to the galley and knew that I would be expected in the Ritz for dinner. As the Boss says, 'Ship life is routine.'

March 26th. Today our Expedition made a scientific discovery, which is a fish caught by Clark that is new to Science.[56] As it happens I know quite a bit about fish and I thought if I saw this one I might be able to tell him if I had ever seen anything resembling it, which could only save him trouble and time down the road. Determined to pay a visit to his lab while everyone was in the Ritz at teatime and finding the door ajar was able to squeeze my way in. In fact, I had never been in here before, Clark being so very proprietorial about his work, and so I had never appreciated just how interesting and intriguing a place it is, full of bottles and jars and shelves and boxes. Jumped up to the workbench and began my investigation of some very disagreeable-smelling bottles, but with things inside them that sloshed and jiggled in a very intriguing manner when knocked or bumped. Was continuing my investigations when I heard footsteps approaching and it occurred to me that this might be one of those places one is supposed to be specifically invited to enter; and just in case, I swiftly ran to the end of

[56]Robert Clark was the Expedition's biologist.

the workbench and jumped down to the floor. I went out as Clark came in, and quickly made my way to the Ritz, where I went under the table and over to my own cubicle, nimbly leaping onto the berth I share with my mate. Suddenly, Clark came striding in, all puffing and excited. 'Anyone seen Chippy?' he asked in a loud, rude, demanding voice. I could hear everyone turn in their chairs and look around. 'Chippy was in my lab and could have smashed my bottles!' he half shouted, as if we were all in the next room and couldn't hear him. I lay very still and listened to everyone shifting their chairs and moving around. A shadow fell over me. 'Chippy's here,' said Cheetham, and picked me up. Hanging from his arm, I blinked sleepily as he carried me towards the table in the middle of the room. I yawned. 'Oh,' said Clark. 'Well, something ran past me from the lab.' 'Could have been a rat,' said Wild. There was a pause. I yawned again. 'Keep your door closed in the future,' said my mate in his growly voice. 'Yes, well, sorry, everyone,' said Clark and left sheepishly for his lab. 'Chippy, stay out of his business,' said my mate that night, as I turned in between his ankles. I wonder how good a scientist Clark really is. Some weeks ago, my shipmates put spaghetti in one of his bottles to trick him; and I catch more specimens in the hold each night than he's managed the whole time he's been here.

March 29th. Watch cut short on account of it being particularly cold. Resumed duties below, in the Skipper's cabin, while he was out looking for seals from the crow's nest. Rejoined my shipmates in the Ritz for tea, sociably rubbing against the line of their big boots under the table. 'Someone had better break the news to Chippy,' said Crean, as I joined my mate on his lap. 'No more butter, Mrs Chippy,' he said. Continued my examination of my mate's plate, and then turned next door to Crean's. 'Sorry, Mrs Chips,' said Crean, 'but there's no more butter.' 'Cookie has us on Merchant Navy rations,' said the Skipper, who was sitting opposite, and winked at Crean. 'No more butter.' This was quite preposterous and I looked up at my mate. 'Aye, Chippy,' he said. 'It's butter only for breakfast now.' I am of course all in favour of sensible restraints and so forth, and in fact would be the first to allow that certain persons have been very greedy, slathering butter on their bread and potatoes, but this does not seem fair to those certain other persons who took only a little lick now and then from what was left over so that it wouldn't go to waste. Tea somewhat spoiled, so I returned to my bowl in the galley, where there was a little bit of milk remaining at the bottom. Reflected that the life of an Explorer is full of routine hardship.

April 2nd. Visited Blackborow in the foredeck, where he and his friends were mending their socks and mittens. Seeing me they all laughed and tucked their wool away in their waistbands and under their legs, to make room for me. In fact, I wouldn't have minded at all if they had kept the wool where it was, as I could have helped them unravel it, as I often have in the past. Joined Blackborow on his bed, and carefully cleaned my ruff and whiskers while my shipmates talked about the Imperial walk, and if it would happen this year, and what their jobs would be.[57] Not everyone will cross Antarctica with Sir Ernest. Blackborow and Cookie will stay in the ship and some of the others will live in a hut on the land. Suddenly, I wondered what my job would be, as Sir Ernest has not as yet said anything to me about going with him. Just as I was thinking these things, McCarthy said, 'I imagine you'll be staying on the ship to help us out here, won't you, Chippy?' That seems to settle it. I can't see much point in lugging all my gear – my bowl and blanket – across Antarctica, especially when my job is so well defined here.

April 9th. Woken early by the humming of our ship and the air buzzing all around us like the flapping of a bird's wing. Putting my ears back

[57]Officially Shackleton made out that he intended to return to the Antarctic continent in the spring, and attempt the transcontinental crossing at that time. Privately, he must have known that the *Endurance*'s inexorable northward drift within the moving pack made this a highly improbable option.

and concentrating hard with the tips of my whiskers and feelers, I detected a vibration travelling to us from far away.[58] Instantly on duty, I hastened up top and found all my shipmates going over the side with their shovels. Assumed watch station at short notice and observed my shipmates as they shovelled and chopped at the ice and growlers, now piled high around us. 'Clear as much of it as you can from the ship,' the Boss called down. 'And we best clear the deck area again, in case the dogs have to be evacuated.' Things now look very ominous.[59]

April 15th. Slept somewhat later than usual, and took my watch around sunset. Things have settled down, and yesterday one of the dogs bit Hudson's nose, so that should keep them on the ice a bit longer. Observed as the sun set twice tonight: first, it sank below the clouds as usual, and then it

[58]The first pinch of pressure from the ice had in fact occurred some days earlier, on 4 April, and it has been speculated that the gentle 'buzzing' vibration it caused, to which Mrs Chippy refers in this entry, may have had a soporific effect on certain members of the crew, causing them to sleep through this earlier disturbance and thus make no mention of it in their journals.

[59]Mrs Chippy's premonitions were justified. As Shackleton recorded, 'the movement [of the ice] was not serious, but I realized that it might be the beginning of trouble for the Expedition' (Shackleton, *South*, p. 44). On this day, the pressure had rafted the ice astern of the ship to a height of as much as eleven feet.

returned and sank again.[60] The Skipper was very excited about this and called out from the crow's nest to Crean who was working on the ice to watch. I generally measure teatime by the slant of the setting sun on the tips of my whiskers; if the sun continues to set twice, I wonder if Black-borow will give me two saucers of milk? It is an interesting question.

April 18th.[61] Things very quiet, winter routine resumed. Observed from the rail as my mate and McLeod went for a little saunter along the ice. 'No, Chippy, best to stay where you are,' he called up from the ice, as I began my descent to join him over the side. 'Chippy can come sledging with me,' Crean called across the ice, seeing my mate turning back towards the ship. 'Now there's an image,' said Macklin, joining Crean. 'Chippy bundled in a scarf, racing

[60]The phenomenon Mrs Chippy astutely observed was in fact the refracted image of the setting sun beamed up, like a mirage, into the atmosphere above the horizon, thus giving the impression of a double sunset. Mrs Chippy's careful record of such phenomena is of great value to Science.

[61]The reader will no doubt remark that increasingly greater intervals of time intervene between the Journal entries. Mrs Chippy was remarkably attuned to the body's natural rhythms and knew that the natural order of the winter season was greater intervals of rest. This kind of self-knowledge and restraint is a characteristic mark of Mrs Chippy's greatness as an explorer. Unlike less self-aware adventurers, Mrs Chippy was not one to indulge in mindless 'heroics.'

through the Polar night.' Others of the sledge drivers began to call out their suggestions until my mate shouted for everyone to stop their chattering and nonsense, and called up to me that my duties lay on board the ship. Observed as my mate strolled away and everyone walked back and forth on the ice. I must say I'm quite interested in going on the ice, the dogs' presence there being proof that it does not require any particular abilities or skills, but it's the sort of thing that should probably be practised once or twice in private, just to be sure. In fact I enjoy this time when the dogs are out being 'exercised' and we are left in peace and quiet. From my rail I can hear the voices of my shipmates in the darkness very acutely and sometimes too the cracking and sighing of the ice. Then there is always a lot of laughing and joking and stamping of feet when the sledgers return and join the other members of the Expedition whose particular jobs entail that they stay on board. After this, we all retire to the Ritz for our tea, which is a very social and comradely time. Continued duties in the galley with Blackborow, who was preparing tea. For all the hardships, I enjoy being an Explorer and would consider undertaking another Expedition.

April 20th. Blizzard blowing and no work outside. Bath day for some of my shipmates, i.e., Crean, with the big wooden basin placed in front of the Ritz stove and filled with hot water.[62] I must say it was a wonderful sight, all steaming and smoking, and the mist rising into such interesting shapes and patterns. As Crean stepped in, I got a little closer so as to have a better look, then Blackborow came from the galley with big pots of hot water, which he poured into the basin on

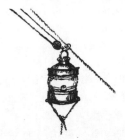

top of Crean. I have always enjoyed watching running water and have passed many enjoyable and instructive hours over a basin or sink, watching the water pour in and flow out. Now I could see the water flow all around Crean's bent knees and observed that every time he moved it made ripples and wrinkles. It occurred to me that if I could just get a bit closer I might able to catch a ripple with my paw, so I got down from the table and went over to the basin and was standing on my back legs stretched up to look over the top. So intently was I watching the water slosh and sparkle that I was not entirely concentrating on my shipmates' voices, and although I heard my name being spoken a couple of times, it didn't seem terribly urgent, so I continued to watch and had just jumped up and balanced myself on the narrow rim, when Blackborow picked me up

[62] All water, of course, was derived from great blocks of ice carved out of the floes and taken on board for melting.

from behind. Clinging to the rim with my paws, I was rudely pulled away and put back on the table. Then I looked around and saw that everyone was laughing. 'The idea!' Crean was saying. 'A man can't take a well-earned bath in peace around here.' 'A cat may look at a king,' said Cheetham. Then Crean clasped his hands together, put them in the basin, raised them and squirted me, catching me on my whiskers, and making me sneeze! Leaping off the table, I ran beneath it to clean and dry myself. Moments later, Blackborow's head appeared beside the legs of one of the chairs. 'Come on, Chippy,' he was saying. 'Our second officer was trying to be clever, that's all.' Reluctantly, I let him pull me out. Crean was out of the bath by now and was towelling off in front of the stove. 'No harm done, eh, Chips?' he said, and rubbed me with his damp hand. I suppose it was all in sport; it is part of the give-and-take of a sailor's rough life. The basin was still warm from the hot water, and when Crean went away to get dressed, I curled up beside it and let it warm my fur. Determined to wait until my mate or Blackborow take their baths to examine things properly. Later, when I was washing myself after dinner, it struck me that my shipmates have adopted a grossly inefficient and troublesome method of keeping clean. I have never been as dirty as most of them are, and I have white stripes that can show marks terribly. Yet I clean myself several times daily without fuss and am always well presented. It is something for future Expeditions to consider.

April 21st. Left a mouse's head on Crean's bed.

April 29th. Pemmican for dinner, which is excellent and proper explorer's food.[63] Joined my mate for a brief constitutional watch while digesting my dinner and considering possibility of racing over the snowfields, at some later date. Snow and ice very hard and white in the moonlight, glinting like teeth. The hills and hummocks look like shining peaks of whipped cream. Reflected that only Explorers witness such sights.

May 1st. All hands on deck to watch a lantern slide show in the sky, the one tonight being better than any we have seen before, very vast and colourful.[64] Everybody exclaimed out loud as the colours swirled and drooped and soared. It was very wonderful, and more enjoyable than the lantern slide shows Hurley gives each month indoors, when everyone always starts shouting at me to move my tail every time I go up to the screen to investigate the colours.

[63] As Mrs Chippy notes, pemmican was a staple of the Polar explorer's diet. It consisted of dried ground meat mixed with fat. Pemmican, water and broken biscuits melted to the consistency of soup was called 'hoosh.'

[64] This is Mrs Chippy's evocative term for the fabled *Aurora Australis*, or Southern Lights.

May 2nd. Slept through dinner last night, and had to get my bowl specially prepared by Blackborow. Was woken by the sound of my shipmates singing and laughing and having a little concert, which is all very well and cheery, if not entirely considerate of those other members of the Expedition who require a little more sleep than others on account of their extra duties. Joined my shipmates briefly, sharing in their merriment and sardines. The Boss called for quiet, saying he'd like to propose a toast. 'To the Sun,' he said, lifting his mug, 'whose light we will not see for the next – how long is it, Hussey?' 'Seventy-nine days,' replied Hussey. 'To the Sun,' said everyone. 'Those of you who've been in these parts know this can be a trying time,' said the Boss, and Crean and Wild and some of the others began to nod very solemnly. 'But we're all of us in the pink of health,' he continued, 'the ship is snug and we've much with which we can occupy ourselves, if we put our minds to it.' I stood up on the table to arch my back, then stretched and yawned and settled down again in front of the Boss, purring loudly. 'Chippy is never downhearted,' said Sir Ernest, smiling approvingly. 'An example to you, boys,' he said and everyone cheered. This fuss about the 'Polar Night' is all a lot of nonsense, and Sir Ernest knows he doesn't have to buck me up on account of a little darkness. Began to doze off listening to the Boss telling the Skipper that it was nice to see that everyone was in such good spirits. I should think that he is very pleased that the Expedition is going so splendidly.

Hurley (left) and Hussey enjoying a game of chess; note open sardine tins in foreground.

May 3rd. A number of penguins caught today, a welcome addition to the Ship's larder. In fact penguins are not proper birds, all stiff and bristly, and nothing like those plump, downy Cape pigeons we saw on the way out, so jolly and friendly and accessible.[65] I was interested to learn that some freshly caught fish had been found inside one or the other of them, and that Clark has taken these to his lab. To bed early, in expectation of Night duties.

May 7th. Tea in the Ritz. Bits of sardine and milk from the bottoms of the cups. I enjoyed the last few days up front with the fo'c'sle hands, but it's nice to be back here, now that the business with Clark and his lab has blown over.[66] My watches all taken belowdecks now, as part of the winter arrangements. I have found that I do need a few more hours of sleep each day, and so out of necessity have had to curtail a number of my activities. I know that the Boss is particularly concerned about keeping strict discipline during these winter months, so I continue to hold rigorously to Ship Routine in terms of observing meal hours

[65]Here as elsewhere one has reason to regret the loss of the Journal's description of the early stages of the Expedition. Mrs Chippy's keen eye for avian life would undoubtedly have been instructive.

[66]Evidently some sort of incident occurred in Clark's lab shortly after the discovery of the fish in the penguin's stomach. Mrs Chippy gives us no clue as to what this might have been.

and so forth, and to make regular inspections of the galley. Learned that the sun whose 'last appearance' everybody made such a fuss about shone again today. I should imagine the scientists are quite mortified.[67]

July 5th.[68] Observed the Skipper making his way up to the crow's nest, where he likes to look out for seals, and realized it had been quite a while since I had kept my own watch there. Scratching my claws below by way of preparation, I looked around to see if anyone was watching me. Bakewell was working by the foredeck and when I saw that I had caught his attention, I sprang up the rigging and nimbly and dexterously made my way to the top, surprising the Skipper as I took my position beside him. 'Hello, Chippy,' he said. 'Come to share the watch?' I had forgotten how very much I like being up there. I could see absolutely everything, all the activity on the ice as well as my shipmates on the

[67]In fact the sun was observed to rise and set a number of times on this day, phenomena that the Scientists rushed to ascribe to 'refraction.'

[68]The length of time between this and the last entry of May 7 has led most scholars to assume that a number of pages from the Journal had been lost. More recent research, including a comparative reading of the diaries of other Expedition members, suggests that Mrs Chippy was occupied with sleeping during these difficult winter days, and had no opportunity to make entries.

deck below. Sniffed the air, which was damp and full of interesting smells, and turned my attention to the dog teams, looking very tiny and insignificant so far below me. Observed that they were continually running into piles of ice, or swerving away from deep cracks and turning over their sledges. It looked very tiresome and wet and I reflected that I had been wise to refuse Crean's repeated invitations to ride with him. Leaning over the edge, I waited until one of my shipmates looked up to see me. 'Heads up!' called the Skipper to the hands below, leaning over the other side of the barrel.[69] 'The First Mate's coming down!' Without wishing to be boastful, it is generally recognized that I am a much better climber than any of my shipmates, and incalculably better than the scientists, who can't climb at all, and everyone enjoys watching me make my way up and down the rigging. I continued to make signs that I was about to come down, until I saw Bakewell look up and nudge How, who called to McCarthy and then they all stood looking up to watch. Down I rappelled, twisting from backwards to headfirst in a single rather difficult move near the end, leaping the last few feet and landing easily inches from McCarthy's feet. He bent down to pick me up, laughing. 'Very nicely done, Mrs Chippy,' he said. I went and sat on a coil of rope and casually

[69]The crow's nest is shaped like an upturned barrel.

cleaned my whiskers. I am not one to lord it over my fellows.

July 6th. A rather unpleasant incident happened today, and I am still a little shaky. I was visiting Blackborow in the fo'c'sle when Vincent came in.[70] I have never liked Vincent. All the trawlerhands are full of puff and swank, but Vincent is nasty, always loud and shouting and pushing everyone around, and I have seen him shove Bakewell against a wall, just to show off. Usually he is never here when I visit, as he likes to stay topside, strutting round the deck, trying to be noticed by the Boss. But since winter came, and since his promotion to Bosun, he's been hanging around more often, usually sleeping with the covers over his head. I could tell when I walked in that it was a bad moment. Bakewell was sitting with his mouth very tight and Blackborow and How were ignoring him. I tried to turn back, but Vincent had seen me, and swooped at me and picked me up. Normally I would have protested against such rude behaviour, but I had a sixth sense that with Vincent it was better to pay no attention, that he would enjoy it if I appeared upset. 'So, Mrs Chippy,' he said in a loud, nasty voice, looking around to see if he had

[70]John Vincent, an able seaman, described by one historian as 'an unsympathetic trawlerhand . . . a blustering bully promoted [to bosun] on the principle, perhaps, of poacher turned game-keeper.' (See Roland Huntford's *Shackleton*, pp. 423f.)

everyone's attention, 'what's this I hear about you provoking the dogs?' He was holding me by the scruff of my neck and I couldn't move. I looked at Blackborow and opened my mouth in a silent meow. Blackborow started to move forward, but How stopped him and they all went back to their work, ignoring Vincent. 'I think you should meet these poor doggies face-to-face,' said Vincent. 'Yes, I think that's an excellent idea. We'll put you down over the side with them and see how you get on.' 'You'd best run that by Chips,' said Blackborow, meaning my mate. Vincent paused for a moment and then said, 'I wouldn't be able to help it, would I, if the wretched animal took it into its head to go snooping around the dogloos? How would that have anything to do with me?' he said, looking around and smirking. It was suddenly very still; everyone was looking at him intently and not saying a word. I felt his hand on my neck slipping, and took a deep breath and swung round with my claws out and freed myself and went straight out the door with my tail high, along the passageway and into the Ritz. I came running in with my ears back and tail fluffed and jumped on my mate's bed. 'Why, what's up with you, Chippy?' asked my mate. But I curled myself up behind his pillow and tried to calm myself and go to sleep. Hanging by my scruff!! In front of my friends!! Stayed on my bunk while my shipmates enjoyed their dinner. My mate got up from the table as soon as he had finished and went out for his constitutional stroll rather earlier than usual, and I decided at the last moment that I would join him. But he did not go topside, but turned towards the fo'c'sle deck. I followed him, then stopped when I saw Vincent coming out of the door. He was looking rather pale and ill and turned back towards his quarters when he saw my mate; but suddenly Blackborow appeared and closed the door behind them. 'I gather you and I have business,' said my mate in his growly voice. He is built like a big tomcat, with wide burly shoulders and an enormous chest, and massive paws from all his carpentry work. Vincent was shaking his head, trying to look confused as if he didn't understand what my mate meant. 'I invited Chips down here,' said Blackborow. 'I thought you might want to tell him the plans you were discussing with us this afternoon — face-to-face.' Vincent was now very white.

He looked from my mate to Blackborow, and then to Bakewell, who had appeared in the passage behind me. Bakewell picked me up: 'You and I are going back to the galley, Mrs Chips,' he said. 'You little sod,' said my mate, in his growly voice, and started moving towards Vincent. I turned to look over Bakewell's shoulder as he carried me away, but I couldn't see anything more. My mate returned to the Ritz a little later, somewhat out of breath, and we both went to bed early. A very unpleasant day. Will I still be able to visit my friends, or has everything changed?

July 7th. Cautiously returned to the fo'c'sle deck after tea. The events of yesterday were somewhat blurred and mixed up in my sleep and dreams and I wasn't really sure how it had all ended. 'Chippy!' cried Bakewell when I came in. Everyone greeted me very warmly, making a very big, rather noisy fuss over me, as I walked from bunk to bunk, swinging my tail. Suddenly, Vincent jumped out from under his bedcovers where he was brooding and hiding, and marched out of the door. Everyone burst out laughing. 'Good riddance to bad rubbish,' said How. I stayed until I was sleepy, and then left for the galley with Blackborow for my dinner.[71]

[71]There is an interesting footnote to this disgraceful episode: Vincent's outrageous treatment of Mrs Chippy was the last straw in a series of unpleasant incidents he had perpetrated. Unknown to Mrs Chippy, a delegation of the fo'c'sle hands went to Shackleton that morning and lodged a formal complaint against the Bosun. Shackleton summoned Vincent forthwith, and while it is not known precisely what he told him, Vincent was a changed man after their meeting – leading one to speculate that the Boss made it clear that if anyone were to be thrown to the dogs, he had someone in mind other than a valuable member of the crew like Mrs Chippy. Vincent was demoted, although his shipmates continued to refer to him mockingly as 'the Bosun.'

July 10th. Today was our monthly weighing. Usually Sir Ernest exempts me from this, knowing as he does how scrupulously I adhere to Ship Routine and how conscientious I am about my bowl, but from time to time my shipmates urged him to verify this properly. It seems there is a little more of me than last time, which is excellent, my shipmates very impressed and pleased. 'Nine pounds 10 ounces,' the Boss announced. 'A substantial gain. No surprises here,' he said, as I stepped off the scales to my shipmates' applause. I am in fact the only member of the Expedition who has consistently made progress in this regard, most of my shipmates even losing weight, which is just bad management. The success of grand endeavours often lies in attention to such details.

July 14th. Blizzard.[72] My shipmates passed the time in telling each other about the other blizzards they have been in, all of them much worse than this one, with those experienced by Francis Hurley being much the worst of all. Wild's account, however, was most interesting and informative. On his last trip to Antarctica, the blizzards were so severe that he was able to get

[72]Mrs Chippy's understated notation is misleading. Of this blizzard, Shackleton wrote that it was 'the most severe . . . we had experienced in the Weddell Sea . . . the ship was invisible at a distance of fifty yards. . . . By evening the gale had attained a force of 60 or 70 miles an hour, and the ship was trembling under the attack' (Shackleton, *South*, p. 54).

outside his tent to feed the dogs only three times in the course of an entire month. In fact, Wild has told this story on other occasions and I have always taken notice of it, as I think there is much to be learned from the firsthand experience of our colleagues on other Expeditions.

July 16th. Blizzard. Spent most of the afternoon in the foredeck with Blackborow and his friends. Bakewell did a very amusing impersonation of Lees counting stores and trying to monitor Cookie's every move. There was more talk about the Imperial walk too, and how far we had drifted. 'Well, Chippy – you'll have a lot to tell your friends when you get home,' said How. 'Chippy the Explorer; Mrs Chippy's Furthest South,' said Blackborow. 'I should imagine they'll give you the Polar Medal.' The Polar Medal! On my whiskers, I never considered honours when I undertook this arduous Expedition; I came out of curiosity and to accompany my mate! And if I have distinguished myself it was only by conscientiously doing those things I knew to be my duty. I went over to where Blackborow was lying on his bunk and standing on his chest began to knead with my paws, all the while gazing solemnly into his eyes. It was a grave and significant moment. Although I have never pursued glory, I would consider it my duty to Sir Ernest and my shipmates of the *Endurance* to accept any honour that might be offered.

July 17th. Sir Chippy; Lord Chippy of Cathcart.

July 21st. Awoken by a fearful noise, like the grinding of teeth and growling of something large and fierce approaching us. I sat up on my bunk, turning my ears in all directions, and watched my shipmates rushing to and fro in the Ritz. All hands spent a lot of time up top, and I thought it best to stay where I was and oversee the 'tween decks. At length, everyone came down and gathered around the table for tea and sardines and toast, which Cookie had specially prepared. The talk was about the unpleasant noises, which the Boss says are due to ice and growlers.[73] The Boss went back up top with Wild and the Skipper, but told the rest of us to stay below and enjoy our tea. My mate gave me part of one of his sardines, which was very oily and smooth on the outside, but with a subtle interior crunch. Clark looked on very sourly as I took the fish from my mate's plate and carefully gnawed it. 'How is it that anything so small can cause so much disturbance?' he said. 'How does it happen that a roomful of grown men can be

[73]Mrs Chippy's use of the casual terminology of an experienced sailor may be unclear to the lay reader. The fierce blizzard of the days before had broken the solid pack into many floes, which, moving independently of each other, created momentous pressure capable of crushing or 'rafting' upwards all that opposed their deadly path. This is the beginning of the period of stress and real danger the ice held for Mrs Chippy and the *Endurance*.

The Watchman returns; Mrs Chippy has just preceded him below.

completely dominated by something that's only –
what? Nine inches high?' 'Force of character,' said
my mate, in his growly voice. Suddenly, everyone
was looking at me. I blinked under the lantern's
warm light. 'More to the point,' said James, 'how
can anything so tiny withstand the pressures of the
cosmos? Snow and ice. The high seas. Only twelve
inches high,' he said, measuring me with his hands.
'But two feet round,' said Crean. 'Mere inches of
life,' said James, his voice rising. 'Against the
momentous weight of Existence. And not just
surviving – leaving a mark!' 'All God's creatures
have what it takes to get by, thank you very
much,' said my mate, 'so long as they're left
alone.' I thought about this conversation later, as
I was going to bed between my mate's ankles. I
suppose I am somewhat shorter in stature than
many of my shipmates, but I can't say I've ever
given this much thought. After all, I've always
found a way to reach anything I wanted to
investigate. Also, James's calculations did not take
into account my tail and whiskers, which are
extensive. Not all of me goes in one direction,
as it does with him.

July 23rd. Slept somewhat later than usual on
account of extensive night duties. I had awoken
some time after midnight to check on my
bowl, and decided to visit the night watchman,
always glad of a little company. Discovered Frank
Wild on duty, smoking his pipe and pacing the

deck.[74] Wild is all right, very predictable and steady, even if he is rather too absorbed with his sledging 'team.' Approached and softly brushed against his boots, then discreetly walked off into the shadows. 'Is that Chippy?' he called. Discreetly emerged from the shadows and then returned to them. 'It's a bit late and cold for you to be out, isn't it, Mrs Chips?' he asked, while I observed his pipe glowing from the shadows. The dogs suddenly began their whimpering and Wild went to the gangway and looked down on them, then came back, having swiftly determined there was nothing at all the matter, they were just making their usual foolish noises. He sat down and sighed deeply, and I emerged discreetly to the edge of the shadows, softly inscribing a circle around him, just out of arm's reach, before coming forward to examine the mug he was holding. 'Tea,' said Wild, holding the mug out for me to examine. He sighed again. 'Only tea,' he murmured. Settling by the ship's rail some distance from his boots, I sat in silence while he smoked his pipe and sipped his tea, listening to the

[74]The ice floe in which the *Endurance* was stuck had cracked from its outer edge to within approximately 120 feet of the port quarter of the stricken ship. In addition to endangering the stores stockpiled on the ice, the break-up of the floe presented the grave danger of possible pressure in the immediate vicinity of the ship. It is significant that Shackleton, Wild and Worsley – the three highest-ranking members of the Expedition – personally took four-hour watches through this night.

cracking of the ice and looking out into the dark. McLeod says it is a Scientific fact that the stars here are two times as big as they are at home, which more or less fits with my own calculations. Remained on watch until the Skipper came stumping across the deck to relieve us. 'Ah, I see Mrs Chippy's keeping you company,' said the Skipper, very heartily, greeting me by scooping me up against his thick jersey. 'Chippy's the watchman's friend, aren't you, Chippy?' he said, rubbing my head. 'But you shouldn't be out in this cold night air.' 'I'll take Chippy below,' said Wild, and I was deftly transferred from our Skipper to our Second-in-command. Accompanied him sleepily over his shoulder to the galley, where he put me in my basket behind the stove.

July 24th. Deck all cluttered with stores and sledges brought up from ice.[75] Things in a muddle and Ship Routine no longer observed. Galley deserted at teatime with nothing prepared. Much, much later everyone came bumping back into the Ritz, where I lay tightly curled on my bunk, attempting to sleep. Ignored Cheetham when he sat beside me to take off his boots.

[75]Those members of the Expedition who had not been up all night on watch duty with Shackleton, Wild, Worsley and Mrs Chippy, busied themselves on this day in preparing emergency supplies for one of the lifeboats in the event of an evacuation.

'Why, what are you sulking about, Mrs Chips?' asked Cheetham. This was very unfair; a quiet attempt to sleep off severe hunger pangs is hardly 'sulking.' Before I could answer, however, Blackborow came in looking especially for me. 'I just want you to have a look at something in the galley,' he said, as he accompanied me out of the Ritz, over his shoulder. 'So,' he said, when we arrived in the galley, 'you've been exploring, haven't you, Mrs Chips?' What could he possibly mean? He held me up and pointed to a line of rather muddy marks that ran around the counter. 'I'd say those look like paw prints,' he said. I looked at them closely; perhaps, one could say, they looked somewhat like paw prints. Conceivably, they may have got there when I attempted to save Blackborow the trouble of having to prepare my bowl by finding my own tea. I struggled to get down. All I had found were biscuit tins, so there was no need for all the fuss and bother, parading me in here etc. etc. Once I got my own footing, I rubbed around his ankles to show that I wasn't upset, and that I would still like to have my tea.

July 26th. Joined my mate and other shipmates in watching the top of the sun rise above the horizon. It only stayed for a minute or two, but the whole company cheered loudly, and indeed I could feel the tips of my whiskers warming. 'Old Jamaica,' said my mate.[76] 'Things will soon be more congenial, Chippy.' I must reschedule my deck watch so as to take advantage of the noon hours.

August 1st. A very alarming day and night. Much agitation outside due to breakup of our floe and evacuation of the dogs from their dogloos. Observed from watch rail as snow-covered dogs were herded meekly up the gangway. 'They're certainly eager to come on board,' said Macklin to the Boss, as they sloped past us. 'They can sense danger,' he said meaningfully, as if this extremely obvious fact were indicative of something remarkable and mysterious. Of course they are 'eager' to come on board. They are fed up with doing the job they were brought here to do and would like to lounge around on the ship again. 'Look out!' cried Hurley suddenly, and the ship suddenly lurched to one side. Clinging to my position at the rail, I witnessed a scene of great horror and devastation as a wave of ice ran through the dogloos, crushing and flinging them into the air – this will almost certainly be used as an excuse to keep the dogs on board. Moments

---

[76]McNeish knew that the seaman's traditional term for the sun would be appreciated by an old salt like Mrs Chippy. The reappearance of the sun signalled the advent of higher temperatures and the eventual breakup of the ice. But as McNeish wrote in his diary, 'we dont want this floe to break up untill there is some open water for it would mean the ship being crushed if we got adrift at present' (H. McNeish, diary, 26 July 1915).

later our ship began to shake and groan, making my fur stand on its very end. Leaping down from my rail, I made my way belowdecks, taking up position in the Ritz until things quieted down and my shipmates came in for a much needed hot drink. Sat quietly with my mate on our bunk while he went through his big bundle, pulling out his Finnesko boots and Burberry coat. 'Just in case, Chippy,' he said. Before we turned in, he took out his photographs of Mrs McNeish and put them inside his Bible. 'Just in case,' he said, as I turned in between his ankles.

August 4th. A most amusing day. Everything is back to normal, except that the dogs are still on board. Ship Routine is reestablished and I had an excellent breakfast, warm milk for tea as well as a lick of Bovril from my mate and Mr Cheetham.[77] All my shipmates are in good humour and we are all enjoying being up top in the new sunshine, busy with our assigned duties. The Boss has reestablished ship watches, which for old sailing hands like ourselves is a comfortable return to routine. The conversation over tea was about how well our splendid ship had stood up to the ice, how we had all pulled through together and how exciting it was to have the sun return and the ice break up and how soon we would be

[77]Bovril rations had been introduced at lunch on 22 June.

sailing again, continuing our Expedition. The Boss joined us as we were discussing these things and, pulling up a chair, he told the following amusing story: There was once a mouse who lived in a tavern. One night the mouse discovered a leaky barrel of beer and he drank all he could hold. And when he had finished, he sat up, twirled his whiskers and looked around arrogantly. 'Now,' he said, 'where's that d – d cat?' I laughed until my whiskers ached! What a very funny story! How exactly it captures the empty bluster of a cocky mouse! That Sir Ernest is a close observer of animal nature has always been apparent to me from the way he keeps an eye on the Expedition members. But I never knew he had such a keen knowledge of mice! I wound my way purring around his boots and my appreciation did not go unnoticed. 'Chips – I think your mate enjoyed that story,' Sir Ernest said to my mate. Wait until I get home and tell Bowser next door! He always enjoys a good mouse story and coming from someone as distinguished and famous as Sir Ernest he will be most impressed.[78]

[78]Shackleton's story was told by way of a warning parable to the Expedition members that overconfidence can be dangerous and that while the *Endurance* had weathered one attack of the ice, others would follow. Although not expressly stating that this instructive point was appreciated, it is unlikely in the extreme that anyone as manifestly wise and perceptive as Mrs Chippy would have missed it.

August 7th. My mate still busy building yet more kennels for the dogs, N.B. their third lot. Left my mate to his duties, the construction of dog kennels being an area in which I have no particular expertise, and visited Blackborow in the fo'c'sle, where everyone was in very high spirits, talking about how nice it will be to be under sail again. I must say, I like the feel of a moving deck beneath my paws, and there is always so much interesting activity when we are at sea, flying, shining water, and all sorts of objects rolling around across the floor. I work much harder when we are under way, but it is good, honest work, necessary to the ship, which I enjoy. On the other hand, I have adapted very well to this more settled winter schedule. Thinking of what lay ahead made me a little restless and I went over to what just happened to be Vincent's locker to sharpen my claws. Blackborow and his friends found this highly amusing. 'I should think that's probably enough, Chippy,' said How, after some minutes had passed. I didn't feel as if I had quite finished, however, and continued to scratch. Blackborow started to get up from his bed and I had a sixth sense he was probably going to ask me to join him, so I left off abruptly, leaping to one side just as he picked me up. As we were going out the door, I saw over his shoulder that I had created a nice burred texture all along the edge of the shiny locker.

August 12th. All of Peggy Lees's petrol burned today in a splendid big bonfire, his little motor-sledge having been officially declared 'useless' in Antarctica. Perhaps this will make him less quick to criticize other persons for doing their jobs.

August 15th. Gramophone night, with Hussey playing along on his banjo.[79] Afterwards, we all turned into bed in high spirits. I snoozed for a little while, then woke and decided to check on my bowl in the galley, as I couldn't remember if I had left it completely empty or not. As it turned out I had, but in returning I happened to pass by the Boss's cabin and seeing that his door was ajar, I cautiously poked my head inside, causing the door to creak open a little wider as I did so. 'Hello?' he called out. I padded inside, rubbing myself against the bed before making my way to the stove that my mate had set up in here to keep the cabin warm. 'Hello, Mrs Chippy,' he said when he saw me in the glow of the stove, 'making the rounds, are you?' I felt a little guilty as strictly speaking I wasn't on night duty, as he seemed to think. He was half sitting up in bed and did not seem to be very sleepy. When we first stopped sailing and ran into the ice, I would often stop by and hear him talking to the night watchman, so I know he is used to not going to sleep. He seemed very pleased to see me and dangled his hand over the edge of his bed. I came and rubbed

[79]Every Sunday, the members of the Expedition enjoyed music on their single gramophone player.

against it headfirst; then turned around and rubbed the other way before returning to the stove. I have always got on with Sir Ernest. Some while ago, when the dogs were first being exercised on the ice, I overheard Crean tell Wild that the Boss had no interest in working with the dogs himself because 'he is not a doggy person,'

which fit my own private assessment. I have been most fortunate to ship on with such a wise and perceptive leader. I was just sprucing up my whiskers when there was a tentative knock on the door, and How poked his head inside, carrying a bucket of coal. 'Stove all right, sir?' he asked. 'Oh,' he said suddenly, seeing me. 'I see you have a visitor, sir.' 'Come in,' said the Boss. 'It's quite all right. I'm sure Mrs Chippy would like you to join us.' How laughed and came in and greeted me beside the stove. 'Well, Chippy,' he said, stroking my head, 'working late, as usual.' 'Yes,' said the Boss, 'one of the more industrious members of our crew. Always up to something or the other.' I felt the tips of my whiskers glow with pride. So my hard work and conscientious efforts have not gone unappreciated! I got up and turned in a circle around How's feet, and then sat down again. 'There was a period, sir, when every time I took my night shift, blame me if I didn't see Chippy either coming or going with a mouse in one stage of disrepair or another,' said How. The Boss laughed, while I pretended to wash my paws. 'Yes, Chippy's untiring,' said the Boss. 'Have a seat, if you have a moment,' he said to How, sitting up straighter in his bed. 'Thank you, sir, I will,' said How, settling down. 'Did you hear about Chippy digging into Lees's private stores?' 'No,' said the Boss, looking very amused. 'When was this?' 'Oh, some weeks ago. It seems that Lees, not to be disrespectful, sir, is in the habit of squirrelling away bits and pieces of his dinner – Nut Cake and chocolate and so on – to eat on his own when everyone has finished theirs. Black-borow was in the Ritz one morning clearing away the breakfast things, when he saw Chippy's tail hanging out from the blankets of Lees's bed. A moment later, Chippy emerged with a mouth full of Nut Cake and skipped off under the table.' This was a very simplistic description of what had been a far more complicated event and I looked anxiously at the Boss, but he seemed to be enjoying the story. 'Sure enough,' said How, 'the next day, when he thinks everyone is busy reading, Lees starts fishing behind his pillow. He can't find what he's looking for, and starts getting a little desperate.' The Boss guffawed. 'Finally, he can't keep quiet, and accuses everyone in the room of stealing his Nut Cake. Of course, Black-borow had told us all what had happened, and everyone swore a blue streak they didn't know what he meant. Wild convinced him it was mice,

Clark and one of his nets.

and he's gone to bed nervously, I should think, sir, ever since.' The Boss laughed very heartily. Luckily, no one likes Lees. How leaned forward to stoke the stove. 'So how are things in the fo'c'sle?' asked the Boss. 'Everyone in good spirits?' 'Yes, sir, I should say, sir. The sun coming back has given us all a lift, so to speak, and we're all looking forward to being on the move again.' The Boss was silent and I absorbed myself with cleaning the very tip of my tail, which is easy to miss. How finished with the stove and said he'd better get back on top. I settled down and although I meant to stay awake to keep the Boss company and continue our earlier conversation, I must have dozed off. And when I awoke a while later, the Boss had gone to sleep, so I quietly returned to my mate's berth. A most rewarding day.

August 16th. Busy on deck this morning, helping Clark and Woodie draw in their scientific nets. Now that the sun has returned, everyone is looking for an excuse to be outside, even those who have no really useful occupations to perform. Greenstreet[80] stopped by to watch me work and seemed very intrigued by my activities: he is not a Scientist and so much of what we were doing was quite new to him. I was busy dragging one of the nets out of the way where I could better examine it.

[80]First Officer Lionel Greenstreet.

The nets are empty but they have very interesting scents which bear a thorough investigation, and also a very nice knotty texture which makes them a pleasure to handle. 'What have you found, Chippy?' he asked, bending over to watch me. 'What have we got here?' He pulled on the net, making it twitch and ripple in a most interesting and provocative way; I followed it a short distance and then snatched it, pulling it back in place while he continued to hold the other end. Clark, who had been hanging over the side of the rail with his other net, straightened up and watched us sourly. Greenstreet winked at him. 'Come on, then, Chippy,' he said to me. 'Better come and help me on the bridge.' I had finished my investigation and so accompanied him under his arm to the other side of the ship, and was soon busy with other pursuits. Later, when we were all gathered for tea in the Ritz, I was amused to hear Clark talking very excitedly about what he'd found in his nets, when in fact I knew they'd come up empty except for some fishy-smelling yellow slime. And now here he was making a fuss about this and how it didn't appear in winter and only when there was sun and so on and so forth. I went over to my berth to thoroughly wash the sardine oil off my whiskers. I would never say as much, because I don't wish to cause any trouble, but it is clear that Clark failed to find fish or real specimens of any kind and so is pretending that the slime is a 'discovery.' I'm afraid I share McLeod's opinion that much of this so-called science is rather bogus. We have been here nearly an entire year, and I am still exactly the same as when I came, as are all my shipmates. So much for Mr Darwin's theory that we'd all 'evolve' into penguins and seals if we were to live for a long period of time on the ice.

August 19th. Slept a little later than usual, and by the time I took my deck watch the sun had already gone in again and the dogs were back on the ship after their exercises. Nevertheless, I made my accustomed rounds, examining all new objects on deck and all objects that showed evidence of having been moved. From a distance, I looked over the kennels, which have cost my mate so much time and trouble to build. My word, these dogs live in the lap of luxury, in their big, solid, spacious doghouses! Having dismissed them from my attention, I suddenly picked up a most intriguing and suggestive scent. Following it first over to where the gangplank comes up on the deck, and then from there a short distance away, I ascertained that at some time in the day fresh penguins had been brought on board. Purring with excitement, I traced the outline of the scent and determined that they must have been taken below. Without the hard evidence of further scents I nonetheless deduced that these would have gone to Clark's lab, so I quickly and quietly made my way there. Clark was in the lab, as it turned out, which made things a bit awkward in terms of a thorough investigation, but I had just enough time on the countertop to determine that the penguins had already been removed. This meant they had been taken to the galley, and that we were going to have them for dinner. Moving swiftly down the passage, ahead of Clark, I swung around the corner into the galley. Sure enough there were Cookie and Blackborow and a pile of penguin skins and a basin full of fresh meat. 'Chippy, you're a bleeding marvel,' said Blackborow. Cookie shook his head. 'It must be telepathy,' he said. I walked urgently back and forth around their feet, looking up and mewing just in case they hadn't completely understood why I had come. 'No!' said Cookie. 'No!' said Blackborow. I began to pace and meow more urgently, seeing that they had failed to grasp my purpose. 'Oh, come on then,' said Blackborow, some minutes later. 'Here – this should keep you happy,' he said, and put a little piece of meat into my bowl. Running over to it, I sniffed it tentatively. It smelt a little tough, a little *worn* – I would say that these were old penguins, or ones in not very good condition. I examined it again and decided that it would be better to wait until dinner time and see what turned up in my bowl then. I looked up at Blackborow to indicate I would not be needing this after all, and then walked slowly out of the door towards the Ritz, waving my tail. Behind me, I heard Blackborow laugh and Cookie swear an oath

– I hope he didn't cut his finger on his skinning knife.

August 20th. A sunshiny and blue day, the sky full of intriguing objects – floating castles and cathedrals, turrets and domes, all in blues and golds and violets, shimmering and shaking like butterfly wings. All hands came on deck to marvel, and the Boss said it was like an Oriental City, or something from Arabian Nights.[81] It was really rather splendid and we all stayed watching until everything vanished with the sun. 'No one will believe us, Chippy,' said my mate. 'When we get home, they'll all say we're telling tall tales.'

August 21st. Slept very deeply, dreaming of the butterfly-coloured city, when I was jolted awake by one of my shipmates rudely drawing back his chair from the table. Not everyone is as considerate of his fellows as one might wish. Having awoken so abruptly, I was a little out of sorts and it took me somewhat longer than usual to get into the swing of my routine. Cancelled my deck watch

[81] The wonderful sights admired by Mrs Chippy were *Fata Morgana* mirages, produced by refraction and enhanced by warm air rising from openings in the ice. Of these Shackleton wrote that 'the principal characteristic is the vertical lengthening of the object, a small pressure-ridge being given the appearance of a line of battlements or towering cliffs' (Shackleton, *South*, p. 60).

Frank Hurley strikes an expeditionary pose with his camera, below the bow of the Endurance.

in the interest of pulling myself together with a snooze and then went into the galley at teatime to see how Blackborow was managing. Went to bed early, trying to recapture my dreams.

August 24th. My word, what a spectacle we had today! Official Expeditionary Photographer James Francis Hurley parading his doggies before his camera, wasting costly cinematographic film which should have been used to record the Expedition! Hurley is always taking photographs of himself in exploratory poses, and when we have group photographs, which I avoid, he tries to get Blackborow to click the camera so he can be in them. This little absurdity apart, a pleasant, rather easygoing day. Breakfast of pemmican. Took several short watches on deck, watched the dogs being exercised from the bridge. The rest of my pemmican for lunch. Worked with my mate. Warm milk tea. Rested in Ritz. Meat stew dinner. Early to bed with my mate. Felt strangely restless around 3:00 A.M., and went to check on the galley. Found Bakewell on night duty and kept him company by the stove, then accompanied him on deck. Night very black, stars very bright. Snow glinting. Ice on my paws, so returned inside ahead of Bakewell and went to visit Blackborow, who was delighted to see me. 'Oh! Lord, it's you, Chippy,' he said, sitting up with a start as I jumped on his bed. He rolled over and drew his pillow over his head, for me to sit on. 'Chippy, for the Lord's sake – your paws are all

Twenty-eight of the twenty-nine members of the Imperial Trans-Antarctic Expedition.

wet,' he said, sounding very weary and despondent. Instantly I began to knead his head and pillow with my paws to show that all was well, and that he mustn't worry about me. I was wet and cold, it was true, but I knew that everything would soon dry off. I curled up by his head and although he was still groaning with concern, was soon fast asleep.

August 27th. A most exciting night. Just after midnight, Greenstreet came into the Ritz with a lantern and called for all hands on deck. Scrambling awake, we all raced up the passageway, with me hard at my mate's heels. Once up top, I stopped at the hatch entrance to sniff the air, which was filled with salty, fishy scents, while my shipmates ran to the rails with their lanterns. Everyone was shouting and peering whereas the Boss and Wild were pointing to the ice ahead of the ship. The air was very black and the dogs were whimpering and yowling like they do every time the ice so much as squeaks, and the smells were so very keen that I felt my fur tingle and my whiskers stiffen with excitement. My shipmates were lit from the lanterns and the stars were in the air and everything felt suddenly so very exciting that I started racing around and jumping onto the coils of ropes and then I galloped towards the lantern shadows. Leaping onto the rail, I saw the ice all sparkling and glittering and then black water beside the ship

The Endurance, *beset, at night.*

where everyone was pointing.[82] At last the Boss told all hands to turn in. I was in the midst of investigating a dark moving pattern on the deck boards, when my mate scooped me up and escorted me below-decks. 'Back to bed, Chippy,' he said. 'No use chasing shadows.' Today everyone is grumbling about being sleepy, while I am as fresh and brisk as ever. I enjoy little diversions like we had last night, when we are all out of our beds sharing an adventure together.

August 30th. The ice has been particularly noisy for the past few days, being exceedingly disruptive at first, although I am now quite used to it. Most of my shipmates have been on deck a great deal of the time, which has made things a little less hectic for me. Took advantage of this extra time to do some spring cleaning. Checked over my blanket and the bunk I share with my mate. Washed myself fastidiously and groomed my claws, pulling off all loose pieces. Ate well and stretched and rested. Feel much better to have caught up on loose ends and ready for the return to my usual demanding routine.

September 1st. The ship made so much noise last night that my shipmates and I did not get much

---

[82]The floe which held the *Endurance* had cracked right under the middle of the ship. If the broken floe had twisted in any way, the results could have been disastrous.

sleep. I am especially tired since I spent a great deal of the night in the storage hold, investigating the effects of the ice noises on the mice. In the early hours of the morning, I brought a present into the fo'c'sle for Blackborow. I had intended to lay it beside his bed, but at the last minute decided to test it one more time just to see if it still worked, and so made a few experimental tosses and so forth. Every-

thing seemed to be in good working order, but unfortunately one of the lockers got in the way and so caused a rather loud sequence of bumps. 'Chippy's got a mouse,' said Bakewell suddenly, from across the  room, in a weary voice. 'You get it.' Blackborow groaned. 'I got the last one,' he said, generously. '*You* get it.' 'It's your mouse,' said Bakewell, gallantly, 'and you know it.' 'Shhh!' said everyone else. I continued to test the mouse, which was still bumping and working very well, while everyone continued to urge Blackborow to take it. Finally, he swung out of bed with a groan and after stumbling around for a few minutes found the mouse where I had left it, and disappeared down the passage. I was suddenly very tired after all my exertions and so got onto his bed. I must have fallen asleep instantly because I don't remember Blackborow getting back in, yet there he was in the morning. I am glad he took my mouse after all, as I feel he deserves it the most on account of his daily attention to my bowl.[83]

September 3rd. More noise in the night, but none of it as off-putting as the noise of our dogs, the Boss himself commenting today on how they have been yowling in a pack at least once a day for the past weeks, and that he is fed up with the row. I have been observing the dogs for some time now and probably have a more objective view of the troubles they cause than do my shipmates, who are out of necessity caught up in the nuisance of their feeding, exercising, etc. In this case, the problem is Hercules, who likes to think of himself as a 'character' and so

---

[83] As often, it is instructive to compare the accounts given by Mrs Chippy's shipmates of these critical days in early September. As the following excerpts reveal, all, without exception, had been badly shaken by the prolonged attack of the ice pressure on the ship. Leonard Hussey wrote, for example, that 'I kept on thinking to myself, "How long can this last? How long?" Such thoughts came most frequently when I was trying to get some sleep . . .' (L. D. A. Hussey, *South with Shackleton*, p. 58). Shackleton admitted to calculating 'that we were 250 miles from the nearest known land. . . . I hoped we would not have to undertake a march across the moving ice-fields. . . . The *Endurance* we knew to be stout and true; but no ship ever built by man could live if taken fairly in the grip of the floes. . . . These were anxious days' (Shackleton, *South*, pp. 61f.). Even McNeish allowed that 'there were times when we thought it was not possible the ship would stand it' (H. McNeish, diary, 4 September 1915). Mrs Chippy's attitude of airy disregard stands in sharp contrast to such ineffectual fretting and is a measure of the cool courage possessed by this remarkable Explorer.

comes up with attention-getting tricks like making a lot of noise. Then all the other smaller dogs follow his example, and the result is this unpleasant wailing 'chorus' which is so irritating and distasteful to the rest of us who are serious Sailors, Scientists and Explorers, and need to be able to concentrate on our work. Yet one has to look at things philosophically. The truth is, it is not really the animals' fault. The kind of sensitive cooperation required for an Expedition of this kind is just not in their makeup. On top of this, their range of abilities is so very narrow that they feel themselves to be – and indeed are – excluded from all the more important and interesting aspects of Ship life. All they are really able to do is haul heavy loads, and they could have done that as easily back where they came from, as they can here.

September 6th. Sunshine today and everyone up top. I was taking my watch in my accustomed place on the rail when I heard the Boss tell Wild and Crean that we should be on the lookout for seals and penguins – apparently the dogs have eaten up nearly all the ship's meat stores!! It is very much like what happened in Grytviken on the way out, when they gorged themselves on whale meat until they became sick.[84] Still, the prospect of acquiring fresh meat is

[84]The name *Grytviken* presents problems of pronunciation to the English speaker, there being no equivalent sound of the Norwegian *y* in the English tongue. For the closest approximation, position your lips as if saying 'cream,' but put your whiskers forward as if saying 'mouse.'

rather exciting, and instead of dwelling on the dogs' greedy appetites I instantly set myself a seal watch. Crouched on the rail in the sunshine and stared intently into the distance, ears cocked, whiskers alert. Tea very welcome. A most strenuous day.

September 7th. Seal watch. The wind arose in the afternoon, and snow began to fall. I enjoy watching the flakes fall through the air, all soft and floating, and in such interesting drifts and patterns, but as in Cathcart I have found that it is more satisfactory to watch them fall from indoors, through a window. Sat for a while in the Skipper's old cabin which has a particularly nice view, then went into the galley, just in case Ship Routine had been changed and Blackborow had decided to serve tea early.

September 9th. Seal watch. Weather still fine and with lots of sun. From experience I know that the best watch places generally lie in direct sunshine, and so I shift my watch accordingly, thus covering many vantage points. My shipmates are very admiring of the way I have orchestrated my watch system. Crean stopped to chat with me today, asking me how things were going, and remarking on how warm my fur was. 'Where's Hussey?' he suddenly called out to Macklin and Hurley and some of the fo'c'sle hands, who were nearby. They pointed aloft, where he had stationed himself with one of his apparatuses. 'We may not need your services any longer,' Crean called up to him. 'Mrs Chippy's minute calibration of the exact position of the sun is better than anything you've pulled off!' Everyone laughed, and I carefully kept my attention focused on the horizon. I like Hussey, although his meteorological methods are rather crude, relying on cumbersome metal instruments and so forth, but I would never wish to hurt his feelings. 'Chippy's equipped with acute temperature sensors,' Crean called up again. 'Far superior to anything you're using.' 'Yes,' Hussey called down, 'but I've noticed they tend not to work so well in extremely cold or wet weather.' Actually, this was inaccurate. My sensors work extremely well in all conditions, but there is rarely any advantage to be gained by exercising them in inclement conditions. Besides, if I were to do so, there would be nothing left for Hussey. I was glad to see he took Crean's pleasantries in stride, however, and when he came down from the crow's nest, he stopped by to greet me and stood at the rail stroking me for a while, looking out over the ice. It occurred to me afterwards that he may have been a little embarrassed by being shown up in front of his shipmates, but he really should not take it to heart. Not everyone is going to be blessed with the same gifts, and I wouldn't be at all surprised to learn that there are one or two things he can do much better than I can.

September 10th. Seal watch. A beautifully warm day. Went out immediately after breakfast with my shipmates. Took up watch position at rail and observed dogs harnessed to their sledges and led docilely onto ice. Decided to focus today on distant ice near horizon. Settled on rail in bright sunlight, i.e., for good visibility. Behind me, I could hear my shipmates laughing and calling to each other as they went about their tasks, and now and then the voices of the sledging parties were carried up from the ice. Suddenly, I became aware that my name was being spoken behind me. Tuning in with half an ear, I realized it was Clark talking to some of my ship-mates. 'Let's see what Chippy makes of *this*,' he was saying. Then there was a *slop slop* noise, which I identified without turning my head as the sound of his wet nets being dropped on the deck. 'Chippy's at the rail, supervising the dogs,' said How. 'Oh, Chippy, Chippy, Chippy,' sang Clark, like a mouse squeaking. 'Chippy, Chippy, Chippy.' I retained my attention on the distant horizon, ears alert for sounds from the ice, whiskers bristling, eyes forward. It is easy enough to watch for seals when they are abundant, but very demanding to do so when none are around, and my task required my full attention. 'I don't think Chippy's interested,' I heard McCarthy say behind me, as Clark continued his squeaking. 'In the past, Chippy's been inordinately interested in everything to do with my nets,' said Clark, rather heatedly. 'Oh, Chippy, Chippy, Chippy.' I continued to keep my attention focused on my own objective. Suddenly, there were

*The dog kennels, showing the line of kennel roofs
used by Mrs Chippy as a convenient watch point
and shortcut along the ship.*

footsteps behind me and I was bodily lifted from my watch post and rudely taken over to where he'd spread his dirty, wet net on the deck, which is against all Ship Rules about not interfering with someone else's job. He began sloshing the net around and poking at a blob in the middle. 'What's this, Mrs Chippy?' he said, excitedly. 'What do you think it can be?' I went over to Bakewell and greeted him, rubbing against his boots; then McCarthy, then How, then Marston. Then I turned my attention to a coil of rope and began examining its nice rough, woolly fibres, all warm from the sun. 'When you think about it, a jellyfish is not really *that* interesting,' said Marston after a pause. 'Well, I'm only delighted,' said Clark sourly. 'Perhaps from now on I won't have to fight for every specimen I bring up,' he said huffily, and began packing up his dripping net. I stretched myself slowly, rubbing against the warm rope, and then strolled off to see what my mate was working on near the bridge. After my tea (milk in galley, sardines in the Ritz) my shipmates teased Clark about this incident. 'You'll have to do better than that if you want to catch Mrs Chippy's attention,' said the Skipper. 'You can't just dredge up any old thing. Can he, Chippy?' he said to me, rubbing my head. My shipmates understand, I think, just how unprofessional this whole business was today. I am afraid that I find Clark a bit of a bore. It's been ages since he's managed to find anything really interesting in his nets, and I suspect the others are as fed up with him as I am.

September 14th. Seal watch.

September 15th. Seal watch.

September 16th. Slept rather later than usual today, on account of past few days of prolonged and intense activity. Strolled out on deck after lunch, making the rounds and conscientiously visiting each of my shipmates and showing an interest in his work. Such socializing is very important to Ship Morale. Visited Hudson and the Skipper on the bridge, where they were discussing scientific and astronomical phenomena. Somewhat later, the Boss came up and the four of us studied the ice, sun, horizon, etc., and made important observations, all necessary to determining exactly where we are. In fact I always know where I am, but Hudson enjoys working through his calculations and having the satisfaction of telling us. Accompanied Sir Ernest down to main deck and joined him in chatting with the fo'c'sle hands. Stayed with them after he left, but resisted invitation to accompany Bakewell to crow's nest, thinking it preferable to supervise my shipmates from the deck, and also feeling a little sleepy. Stationed myself on coil of warm rope. Was woken by raucous noise of dogs returning from their exercise. Watched them led up the gangplank and chained to their kennels. Yawned, stretched and walked towards the wheelhouse, taking shortcut over kennel tops, where I joined my mate, who was just putting away his tools. Accompanied him under his arm into the Ritz for tea. Short snooze before dinner. To bed early. Another full but satisfying day.

September 17th. Slept rather later than usual on account of warm weather. Went on deck to find Clark talking excitedly about his nets which he had spread out on the deck covered with more yellow slime. Walked straight across them on my way to my watch, shaking my paws free of the drops of water I picked up as I did so and stationed myself at rail. Blackborow came up to enjoy the weather with basket of potatoes, and I went over to help him rub off the sprouts. I am not at all proud about helping a shipmate with lesser duties, and am always eager to be of assistance, for example, in the galley. Remarked to myself how this warmer weather has somewhat slowed down my routine. Awoke in the galley, on basket behind stove. Indicated to Blackborow that my bowl was empty. 'You've had your dinner, Mrs Chippy,' he said. I continued to look up at him, as he bent towards me. 'I brought you in when the sun went down and gave you your dinner then. See,' he said, tipping my bowl, 'there's still some gravy from the stew.' I studied the bowl carefully. A picture came into my mind of my whiskers bristling over a full, warm bowl, but I couldn't remember if that was from yesterday or today. I looked up again at Blackborow. 'No, Chippy. You've had your dinner,' he said. I didn't want to upset Ship Routine, but on the other hand it didn't seem very fair if I couldn't remember enjoying my bowl. I sat down with my paws neatly together and, looking up, meowed silently. Blackborow drew a big sigh. 'This isn't a restaurant, you know, Chippy,' he said, going to the stove. 'Just this once,' he said, adding a little something from his big pot. Purring loudly, I addressed myself to my bowl. I think I was justified in my persistence, as it is always best to be safe in matters of health and diet. Sir Ernest has been very concerned about the ship's well-being and I know he would be dismayed if he were to learn that a member of his Expedition was undernourished.

September 20th. Slept rather later than usual for the past few days, on account of the increase in my duties. The fact that I have been on seal watch has not diminished any of my other responsibilities and so I have essentially been doing double duty. My efforts have not gone unnoticed, however, and almost all the ship's company has stopped by at one time or another to greet me and chat while I am at my watch post. Invariably, everyone comments on the wisdom of my choice of station. Bakewell remarked today how the places I select are always some twenty degrees warmer than anywhere else on the ship. Crean stopped by and lowering his head beside mine tried to follow my gaze. 'What *is* Chippy looking at?' he said. 'Something must be out there, but blame me if I can see what it is.' I continued to keep my focus, unfazed by these rather unprofessional attentions. Keeping watch properly means being prepared to give one's complete attention to what may not yet be there. Broke my watch just before teatime and went to the other side of the deck to meet my mate. Helped him pack up his tools and accompanied him to the Ritz. During tea, Hussey was once again chided for his relatively poor meterological skills. 'I've thought of an interesting project for you,' the Skipper told him. 'Why don't you chart on an hourly basis the temperature of Mrs Chippy's ever-shifting places and compare the results with the mean temperature of the rest of the ship?' A number of my shipmates laughed. 'It would make a fascinating paper for the Royal Geographical Society,' Wordie agreed. To his credit, Hussey was very good-natured about the suggestion. 'I might find the magic formula,' he said, rather wistfully I thought. 'Length of feelers times angle of sun divided by whiskers.' Everyone laughed at this foolishness. Still, I am not at all proprietary about my work and would be only happy to contribute to a learned study of the kind Wordie suggests.

September 23rd. Penguin on ice! A most exciting day. The penguin popped out of the ice and was making its way along the floe ahead of us when it was spotted by one of the greedy dog teams returning from their exercise. Instantly, pandemonium broke out. Running in an uncontrollable

Mrs Chippy assists Cookie with the skinning of a seal (note paw helpfully extended by Cookie's ankle).

pack, totally disregarding the orders of their leaders and even upsetting their driver, they attacked the animal and savaged it. The team drivers were jolly angry as well they might be and had to lay into the dogs on the ice. I watched intently from the rails, my fur raised in disgust at this horrifying display of wilful insubordination. Disregard of the commands of superior officers is an extremely grave offence and I wouldn't be surprised if there were not very severe consequences to be paid. The penguin was retrieved, but it is ruined for Science. I felt very badly for poor Clark, who works so hard to obtain specimens, labouring for hours with his nets on the ice, only to have this choice penguin snatched away. I watched while the dogs were brought back on board and after they had been securely chained I took a little stroll to the wheelhouse, across the kennel tops. My word, what a lot of noise! I paused midway to clean the tip of my tail and to look out over the ship, enjoying the vantage point. Was greeted by my mate, who snatched me from the last kennel roof. 'Chippy –' he said in his growly voice. Somehow, I didn't think it wise to respond, but accompanied him without resistance under his arm to tea.

September 24th. Seal!

September 26th. Seal!

September 27th. Finished supervising storage of seal meat and blubber. Seal liver in my bowl and all my shipmates in good spirits, so evidently my long watches paid off. Yesterday, I received each meal exactly one hour earlier than usual, which is a very good adjustment of Ship Routine to Ship Morale.[85] Everyone was most impressed that I was at my bowl for breakfast this morning at the correct time, having adapted readily to the new schedule. 'It really is quite uncanny,' Cheetham remarked at breakfast. 'How do you think Chippy knew?' I strolled away, appearing later exactly on time for lunch. All hands spent most of the day on deck, watching and listening to the ice which is making a lot of noise. Briefly joined the sailors up top, who commented that the ice sounds like the roar of the sea.

September 30th. A most disruptive day. Everything in turmoil, the ice roaring, my shipmates rushing around, dogs barking and the ship shaking and bending. Was sitting quietly in the Ritz in anticipation of tea when the ship suddenly lurched, the ceiling beams bent and snapped, and everything was filled with a terrific grinding and groaning noise. Everyone went dashing up top, while I stayed where I was, with my fur on end. Much shouting and stomping overhead, my mate

[85]Shackleton notes in his journal that the ship initiated a daylight-saving system on 26 September.

nowhere in sight, and no clear orders given as to whether I should stay or go up top. I put up with this for several minutes, waiting for some sort of explanation, and then eventually gave up and curling myself tightly on my berth went to sleep. Was woken a little later by my shipmates returning to the Ritz for their tea. Apparently, all the fuss is over and Ship Routine has not been disrupted. It struck me that the whole business was rather badly managed. This shaking and growling has happened a number of times now, always accompanied by a lot of running around and lack of order, and there is no longer any excuse for this sort of muddle. I continued to lie tightly curled on my bunk, only bothering to raise my head as tea was served. For reasons difficult to fathom, my shipmates seemed to find my evident disapproval rather amusing. 'Chips, I think your mate is out of sorts,' said Hussey to my mate. 'Mrs Chippy's looking a little peevish.' Everyone turned to look at me, some making personal comments about the particular tilt of my ears and whiskery expression. I got up, arched my back and turning round settled down again, facing the back of my berth. 'Chippy doesn't like confusion,' said my mate. 'No more do I.' Joined my shipmates some moments later, where a little piece of sardine was waiting for me. 'There now, Chippy,' said Cheetham, rubbing my head. 'We'll try very hard not to let this happen again.' I finished licking the sardine oil off my whiskers, and decided to let this incident pass. Everything considered, they probably did the best they were able, but the whole muddle showed a remarkable lack of planning.

October 1st. This morning after breakfast examined the galley stores and shelves with Blackborow. Found many things in disarray from yesterday's muddle and had a thorough reorganization. Examined minutely all tins and boxes, picking up many interesting scents. Expressed a keen interest to examine the upper storage shelves, near the ceiling. Standing on lower shelves, I stretched my head up to look and began to explore a route of ascent by way of intervening shelves. 'There's nothing much up there, Chippy,' said Blackborow. 'Only a lot of tins.' Continued to investigate a route of ascent, manoeuvring onto shelf above and displacing a number of objects, which I closely observed as they fell to the floor. 'Here you go, Chippy,' said Blackborow, with something of a sigh. Extracting me from my new, elevated station, he placed me upon his shoulder, allowing me to examine closely all the upper storage shelves at close range. This was a most interesting and diverting task and enabled me to clear up many questions I have had for some time about a variety of intriguing but out-of-the-way objects. Purring loudly, I sniffed at every shelf, sometimes putting a paw up to indicate to Blackborow that I would like him to stop so I could examine something more closely. Our inspection concluded, he lowered me to the floor. Entered spare potato pot to reflect upon what I had seen. It is most satisfying to know that I know exactly what's what, and where everything is.

October 2nd. Breakfast. On deck for watch. Very misty and rather damp, so returned to galley and new place in spare potato pot. Returned for second watch after lunch and found everything blue and sunshiny. Examined deck minutely, noting that it has become rather wavy in places.[86] Observed as my shipmates moved a number of objects on the deck back to their old places, and minutely examined each object after they had finished. Found my watch rail bent, but not at all uncomfortable. Observed that the doghouses were comically askew. A diverting and varied day.

October 6th. By all reports, it has been rather cold and misty outside over the past few days. Devoted myself to ensuring everything was shipshape in galley, after our reorganization. Decided this afternoon to take a little airing, and so briefly left my duties in the galley to go up top with my mate. Found many of my shipmates watching the ice steaming like a saucepan of hot milk.[87] Sniffed

[86]The brief but fierce attack of the ice on the last day of September had actually caused the decks to buckle.
[87]The 'frost smoke' rising from open cracks in the ice was a clear indication of the long-awaited breakup of the pack. Pools of open water and leads now lay all around the *Endurance*, although the ship itself was still pinned by the floe that had trapped it all winter.

the air intensely, ears back, whiskers forward at this spectacle, while my mate held me at the rail. There was so much steaming and smoking that my shipmates were almost hidden from sight. From time to time, the Boss would come into view a little beyond us, pointing to plumes of smoke coming out of the big cracks in the ice and saying how they looked like steam engines. Remained at rail with my mate until the damp began to penetrate my fur. Seal in bowl now for every meal.

October 10th. Woke early and was out before breakfast to enjoy a particularly warm and sunny day, full of interesting scents and noises.[88] Took up position at my watch rail and observed a variety of animal life on the ice. Was joined later by my shipmates, who commented on my early diligence, remarking that I had not yet even had my breakfast. At noon, my shipmates removed their hats and their jackets to enjoy the sun. Distracted by a sudden snuffling and whining from the dog kennels, my shipmates and I turned to discover that the dogs were looking very woebegone and bedraggled from the melting ice that had dripped

[88]Mrs Chippy's meteorological gifts were unerring. Ship records indicate that the temperature rose to nearly thirty degrees Fahrenheit on this day, allowing Mrs Chippy and the other Expedition members to enjoy the warmest weather in seven months.

onto them from their kennel roofs. Strikingly, these big, well-fed animals, with their thick fur and ironical names like 'Samson' and 'Hercules,' are greatly affected by this slight change in their circumstances! Decided that the most constructive course of action was an examination of the kennel roofs, and so nimbly made my way on top, discovering them to be entirely clear of snow and indeed very pleasantly toasty. Exercised my claws by prolonged scratching on the roofs, ignoring the terrific din that erupted from below. 'Chippy!' shouted Macklin, running towards the kennels. 'Chippy!' Stretched and settled down, enjoying sunshine. Watched as Macklin and McIlroy waded in amongst the dogs, who were now fighting each other, slipping and sliding in the slushy snow and falling against their chains.[89] Turned my attention to the ice, watching intently for seals. Stretched again and yawned, then carefully washed my paws. Observed that Macklin had to stun Satan with an uppercut to his jaw, and that McIlroy was holding two dogs at arm's length by their throats. Was just preparing to lean forward for a closer look, when my mate's hands closed around my tummy. Rudely pulled from my watch station, I was carried over his head towards my shipmates, who had been observing the kennel ruckus from the rail with great amusement. Struggling free, I

[89]Dr James McIlroy was, like Macklin, one of the ship's surgeons.

scampered aft to the wheelhouse, having a sixth
sense that this was one of those occasions when
my actions would be twisted around and mis-
understood.[90] My mate and I are now back in our
old cabin.

October 12th. An excessively busy few days, my
mate and I disassembling the winter arrangements,
as we are now moving from the Ritz to our old
cabins, which took many hours, i.e., tracking loose
nails, examining interesting items that came to light
as everything was shifted. Weather particularly
warm, so maintained rigorous watches at my rail
throughout the day, rushing back and forth from
the Ritz to the deck along the narrow passageway.
'Chippy, why don't you either go in or stay out?'
asked Marston as I passed him for the tenth time that
day. Passed Lees who was carrying an enormous pile
of his possessions to the cabins and not looking

[90]Leonard Hussey, writing thirty-four years after the events,
recalled that Mrs Chippy 'was very fond of walking along the
tops of the dog-kennels, just out of reach of the dogs . . .
[Mrs Chippy] trotted along most disdainfully and almost
teasingly, ignoring [their] terrific shindy . . .' Hussey goes
on to speculate that Mrs Chippy enjoyed 'flaunting' this
freedom to the chained dogs (L. D. A. Hussey, *South with
Shackleton*, p. 40). Clearly the intervening years have somewhat
garbled Hussey's memory of events and he has confounded
Mrs Chippy's undoubted enjoyment of the fulfilment of ship
duties with something more personal. Hussey's befuddled
reminiscence underscores the historian's need to bring care
and circumspection to the study of even historical documents.

where he was going and so got caught up in my paws and took a fall. Continued on my way up top and assumed position at my rail, close to where some of my shipmates were gathered, enjoying the noon sun. Was having my head rubbed by Hussey when Lees stumbled on deck and began saying rude things to me. Turning my head, I gazed at him briefly, then turned back to my watch, attention fixed intently on the ice. Lees knows jolly well that I have to use the passage to get to my watch rail, and if he were not so antisocial he would be more aware of the other person's movements. Spotted a distant seal and cocked ears forward as Lees left grumbling. 'So, Chippy,' said Hussey, lifting me from the rail. 'I hear the Colonel took a tumble.'[91] And suddenly turning me on my back he tickled my tummy, while I purred and snatched with my paws at his hands. We sailors are a rough-and-ready, rumble-tumble lot! 'Old Lees,' said the Skipper, who was nearby, 'scurrying off ahead of everyone to nab the best berth, his clothes all neatly folded, as you may be sure —' 'Earnest, anxious, preoccupied,' interjected Greenstreet. '— meets his comeuppance in the furry form of the ubiquitous Mrs Chippy!' Everyone laughed very heartily, and even Clark, who was in earshot, smiled rather sourly. 'Yes,' the Skipper continued, 'Chippy is the great equalizer. We are all mere Men in the eyes of God and Mrs Chippy.' I remained with my

[91]'The Colonel' was yet another of the unfortunate Lees's nicknames.

friends some moments longer, enjoying this sailorly camaraderie, then remembering my duties to my mate and all the rolling nails and intriguing piles of lumber in the Ritz, I struggled to get down and hurried away below. Passed Lees in passage, limping, and was soon at my mate's side, lending my paw where I was able. Had a quick bowl of milk for tea, then back to cabins. Burrowed under a blanket on Cheetham's bed and waited to be discovered. Hasty dinner in the galley, then back to the Ritz, now abandoned and in darkness. Sat very quietly, listening. Was rewarded by the faint rustle and *scratch scratch* of displaced mice, relocated to the hold along with the newly moved stores. Padding softly towards the sounds, reintroduced myself to mice by way of indicating to them that nothing had changed in terms of our relationship. Moused late into the night, getting to bed between my mate's ankles in the early hours of the morning. Although it didn't strike me at the time, I was jolly lucky not to have been seriously injured when Lees tripped over me.

October 14th. A very blustery, cold day. Went up to take my watch, but realized on reaching threshold of upper deck that conditions were not conducive to good visibility. Returned to galley and examined my bowl, finding it still empty, as I had left it. Entered potato pot for a brief nap. Came out for tea, and then later again for dinner. Realized that

The Endurance *in the pride of her youth.*

the sleep deprivation of the past few days has at last caught up with me and resigned myself to the fact that I must attempt to make up these lost hours. Reentered potato pot, reflecting that there are times when one is wise to acknowledge one's limits.[92]

October 15th. Slept rather later than usual, on account of excessive fatigue, waking just before teatime. As dinner was only a few hours away, it seemed pointless to initiate any major project at this time. Had my tea, stretched, and relocated to basket behind galley stove.

October 17th. Slept rather later than usual, waking after lunch today, and not at all yesterday. Enjoyed a full bowl of seal liver and sauntered out to take my

[92]On this day the *Endurance* came free of the floe which had held it all winter so that, while still surrounded by threatening ice, it floated free and clear on open water for the first time in nine months – a situation that was both dangerous and held promise of an early breakout. The fact that the Journal omits any reference to this important event has been taken by some would-be historians to imply that this event went unremarked by Mrs Chippy. Such so-called scholarship which purports to draw conclusions from isolated incidents without reference to circumstance or context – in this case Mrs Chippy's redoubtable powers of observation and deep interest in all matters concerning ship life – does a grave disservice to the task of the serious, dispassionate scholar of history. In fact, the omission of so significant an event at this time is an eloquent indication of the extent to which Mrs Chippy had been absorbed by an extraordinarily wide range of taxing duties.

watch. Enjoyed many warm places of good visibility, and received greetings from my shipmates. Was amused to observe frenzy of dogs at the common sight of a penguin! My word, it doesn't take much to set them off![93] Shortly afterwards, the Boss gave orders to set the sails. What excitement! I leaped off my watch rail to come to the aid of the deckhands as they unfurled the crinkling, rustling, twitching canvas, trailing its interesting pieces of rope. 'Heave ho!, Chippy,' called Bakewell. 'Best let that go, or you'll be run aloft!' Up went the sails, thumping and cracking in the wind, jangling all the wires and ropes. Back and forth my shipmates called to one another while I raced around on the foredeck, the wind bristling my whiskers, and all the while the poor chained dogs could only look on. There is nothing like the sailor's life! Later, we took the sails down again and returned for tea. The ship began to make noises, the old grinding, groaning, hammering etc. etc. While my shipmates rushed up top, I settled on my mate's bunk and enjoyed a short snooze before dinner.[94]

[93]Mrs Chippy was not exaggerating. As Captain Worsley himself humorously noted, 'the dogs are kept in a state of uproar by the sight of so much game, & when the Emperors give vent to an apparently derisive "Knark," they appear on the verge of insanity' (F. A. Worsley, diary, 13 October 1915).

[94]This famous passage was singled out by the great explorer Sir Hartley Puhrgh, C. M., as 'most perfectly embodying those qualities that made the great years of British exploration truly Golden.' He writes: 'The subtlety of description and cool understatement of the fearful events narrated in the course of

October 18th. A very interesting day. As it was rather snowy and wet this morning, I was forced to cancel my watch, on account of visibility. Caught up on sleep until lunch, then visited Blackborow in the galley and returned with him for a little socializing in the foredeck. Caught up on more sleep on his sweater and accompanied him back to the galley for my tea. Having completed the first part of my tea, I joined my shipmates in the wardroom for a little something extra, i.e., sardines on toast.[95] I had just settled myself on a book Wordie was reading, when suddenly, without any notice, we were all turned on our sides! All the tea things went sliding off the table, all the chairs overturned, all my shipmates and I were tumbled together. I fell into Lees's lap

---

these fateful days is scarcely to be credited.' The lay reader must turn to the words of other members of the Expedition to apprehend the full horror of their circumstances. Captain Frank Worsley, writing some fifteen years after the events, allowed that he could still 'feel the thuds and shocks as distant floes drove heavily against those near to us and can hear the noise made by the snapping of the floes as large pieces would break from their impact with the ship. I can hear too the dreadful grinding and scraping . . .' (F. A. Worsley, *Endurance*, p. 8). Sir Hartley continues: 'Mrs Chippy's almost total disregard for the diabolical forces at work upon the ship is more than remarkable – it is inspirational. Such perfect courage is, alas, not to be found in our modern age' (H. S-J. Puhrgh, *Tails of Courage*, p. 117).

[95] After the abandonment of the Ritz, Mrs Chippy's shipmates resumed taking their meals in the restored wardroom. Mrs Chippy's own Ship Routine continued to be observed in both the wardroom and galley.

The ominous list to port.

and only by fully extending my claws was I able to hold on and right myself. Everyone scrambled and crawled up top, while I raced ahead of them, having quickly regained my balance. What a sight met us! One line of kennels had crashed  into the other and all the dogs were tangled together, caught up in their chains, fighting and tearing at each other, slipping and sliding and howling in terror. I put my ears back and observed from a distance as Wild and Macklin and the other dog handlers crawled into the fray! The Boss was shouting orders, and the Skipper was hanging over the low side of the ship looking at the ice. My shipmates began crawling along the deck slope, gathering things together. I raced along beside them, leaping onto the rail, and examining the lifeboats that were almost touching the ice. Alighting onto the back side of one of the overturned kennels I easily kept my footing, and observed my shipmates as they tried to untangle the panic-stricken, terrified dogs. Adroitly leaped down and joined the Skipper at the port side, then scampered off to help the sailors who were untangling ropes. Settled down to watch with very close attention as Lees and some of my other shipmates crawled along the deck on all fours nailing pieces of wood onto the deck.[96] Sniffed each piece of wood with great attention and chased the nails as they rolled down the deck. Was absorbed with apprehending nails until dinner. On returning to the galley, I was somewhat taken aback to discover that the stove fire had been allowed to go out! This wasn't at all like Blackborow and I began to be concerned that something might be seriously wrong with the ship. However, my bowl was prepared as usual, although in a somewhat awkward place. Finished my bowl and joined my shipmates in the wardroom, where they were sitting on the floor with their dinners, conveniently close to my own level. 'Mrs Chippy!' Crean greeted me. 'What fun, eh?' I understood this greeting to be an invitation to examine his bowl, but apparently it was not. 'Here's a quiz,' said the Skipper from the opposite end of the room. 'Name the one sentient being on this ship utterly unaffected by its near capsize?' 'Mrs Chippy!' came the reply, in a chorus of voices. I passed from one of my shipmates to the next, rubbing against their knees and investigating their bowls. Settled down on my mate's lap to enjoy the conversation of my shipmates. A short while later, we were all suddenly slid back to upright! Everyone got up again and knowing it would now be only confusion I betook myself to my cabin and settled on our bed.[97]

[96]These were battens, nailed to the deck to provide footholds for all those less surefooted than Mrs Chippy.
[97]The *Endurance*'s thirty-degree heel to port had been caused by the pressure of a floe on the starboard bilge and the collapse of the floe on which the port side was resting. When the floes opened, the ship was righted.

October 19th. Woke shortly before midnight with the uncomfortable feeling that I might have left something over in my bowl. Made my way to the galley and verified that it was indeed empty. Was struck by sudden thought that if everything in the ship had been disturbed by the tilt, many things in Clark's lab would also have changed their positions, such as, say, those interesting bottles and also penguin pieces. Quietly padded down darkened passage to the lab. Found door ajar but with a light shining inside, meaning someone was in there. Gently pushed my head through the crack in the door, making a faint noise that caused Clark, who was arranging things on his counter, to turn in the lantern light and look down at me with a start. I looked at him, he looked at me. I began to rub the side of my face against the door frame. 'Well, Chippy,' he said, 'what keeps you up so late, hmm?' I continued to rub my whiskers against the door frame, then walked softly over to Clark and wound my way against his legs. I could just see that in fact all the bottles were more or less in their old places on his counter, so there didn't really seem any point in an investigation. Wound once more against his legs, then softly padded out, leaving him watching me in silence. Pricking my ears in the passageway, I heard the voices of my shipmates up top and realized that everyone was working very late. Heard interesting noises coming from the boiler room and seeing that I still had some time on my paws I made my way there. Found Rickinson and Kerr busy pumping up the boiler, which meant they were going to light the fires. 'Hello, Chippy,' said Kerr. 'Come to lend a paw? We haven't had you down here in a while.'[98] Settled in front of boiler to wait. Dozed off and was woken by sound of boiler heating up. Remained at my station in front of boiler for most of morning, observing it heating up. Bunked with Blackborow, on his pillow.

October 20th. Apparently my shipmates have found the late-night shifts of the past couple of days rather trying and everyone is looking a little creased and wrinkled. I was up late too, of course, but appeared brisk and fresh at my breakfast bowl, my whiskers stiff and bristly and my fur unrumpled. The Boss conducted a lengthy and extremely important talk with my mate and me today, regarding the building of a little boat, and we have been occupied most of the day accordingly, while everyone else takes turns watching the ice.[99] Worked

[98]Louis Rickinson and A. J. Kerr were the Expedition's engineers. The boiler fires had not been lit since the ship had been trapped in the ice nine months earlier. Shackleton ordered all loose timber to be cut up to fuel the fires, so as to get up steam. While the movement and breakup of the ice presented real danger to the ship, it also gave rise to the hope of an opportunity to steam through to freedom. As Shackleton wrote, 'The *Endurance* was imprisoned securely in the pool, but our chance might come at any time' (Shackleton, *South*, p. 71).

[99]Shackleton asked McNeish to build a light punt, with the view to navigating any channels that might open ahead of the *Endurance*. In many respects, as became increasingly clear, the fate of Shackleton and his Expedition members lay in the hands and paws of the carpenter and his mate.

with my mate on the aft deck, measuring wood and selecting nails and, as the hours wore on, sitting close beside him out of the wind, so as to be ready at a moment's notice should he require my assistance. Between lunch and tea I observed the boiler fires, which are working splendidly. To bed early between my mate's ankles.

October 21st. Slept rather later than usual over the past two days, on account of the drop in temperature which forced me to cancel my watches. My shipmates are coming and going at all hours, in and out, in and out, and we are never all of us in the same place at the same time.[100] Still, this means there is always someone below to converse with, or share a cup of grog and so forth, and it has been rather a pleasant time. My shipmates are, generally speaking, a sociable crew and, generally speaking, they willingly share a little something with a fellow seaman, i.e., sardines, milk from the bottoms of their cups and so forth, and so the new system works very well. My shipmates come and go, while I remain here, keeping everything toasty and warm for their return. Sat on my mate's lap while he wrote his diary after dinner;

[100]Mrs Chippy's observation is correct. Shackleton had resumed a regular sea-watch schedule – four hours on deck, four hours below – in the event that a lane appeared in the shifting ice, enabling the *Endurance*, now with boilers stoked in readiness, to escape.

The trapped Endurance, *seen from the pressure-stricken ice, a vantage point wisely avoided by* Mrs Chippy.

then sat on his diary, so as to share his thoughts.[101]
To bed between his ankles.

October 23rd. Up for my usual watch, despite
somewhat uncomfortable wind. Was greeted
warmly by my shipmates at my rail. 'There really
is something indescribably comforting about seeing
Mrs Chippy crouching at the rail as usual,' I overheard James say to Marston, and even Clark, who
was nearby, nodded sourly. 'It gives everything an
air of normalcy.' Although I felt my whiskers
glowing, I did not turn my head or behave in
any foolish prideful manner, but focused more
intently than ever on the ice, especially on a
penguin I had noted in the distance. Today would
be a good day to go on proper seal and penguin
duty, but everyone seems only concerned about the
ice immediately around us, and it is left to me to
keep an eye on things further afield. Relaxed my
watch and joined my mate, assisting him in the
building of our little boat. Tried to engage my
shipmates in a game of rope hunting, but everyone
is only interested in the ice. Strolled onto the bridge,
greeting Wild, Worsley and the Boss by winding
respectfully in and out of their boots. Worsley
picked me up and stroked me for a few minutes.

[101]McNeish's words in his diary this night were: '. . . very quiet
but tonight there looks as if there was going to be a bit of
pressure' (H. McNeish, diary, 21 October 1915).

In fact everyone is being cuddly today,[102] Caught sight of Blackborow leaving for the galley and struggled down, so as to accompany him. 'It must be lunchtime,' said the Boss, observing my punctilious departure. It is very gratifying to know that our Expedition leader is aware of how scrupulously I maintain Ship Routine. Snoozed by galley stove until teatime, then pulling myself together set off on a lengthy mouse patrol. Returned for dinner. Slept in the fo'c'sle with Blackborow, for whom I brought a gift.

October 24th. Calm, bright morning. Breakfast of seal. After checking that all the fires were going well, went up top for my watch. The ice was moving a great deal, making it difficult for me to make clear sightings. Observed as the ice rose up in places and burst open, just as if a whale had smashed through it, only there wasn't one. Noted the onset of inclement weather by tingling in tips of whiskers and hastened below, settling in wardroom on my accustomed chair. An hour later, my ship-mates returned for lunch, covered with snow. 'We should have come in when you did, Chippy,' said Cheetham. 'How does Chippy *always* know when

[102]This is a fascinating insight. Modern studies have confirmed the enormous psychological benefits to the listener of a purr, a fact Mrs Chippy's shipmates had apparently instinctively grasped.

bad weather's coming?' After lunch, took a short break in the potato pot until teatime, and then again at dinner. Joined my shipmates in the wardroom for dinner, supplementing my own meal with a little something here and there, to help ward off the cold. Was just going to join my mate on his constitutional stroll when we were all violently shaken and an odd and very unpleasant screaming noise arose from the ship. My shipmates froze, then rushed above. Left alone, I first examined my shipmates' bowls, just in case they had wasted anything, then decided to join them up top. Found everyone in great disarray, running around and pointing and exclaiming at the ice. Many of my shipmates looked pale and shaky, rather like they do when they are going to be seasick, leading me to wonder if we were going to be under way again. Joined Macklin, the Skipper and Hussey at the rail. 'I don't believe I have ever before been made so aware of the colossal forces of Nature,' said Macklin in a solemn voice. Leaping to the rail, I saw that all the ice was rippling, like a great but slowed-down wave coming towards us. Checked ice intently for seals, but saw none. I have always known about the 'colossal forces of Nature,' i.e., rainstorms that soak my fur, and all the shifting seas,[103] so I was not surprised. I thought all proper Explorers knew this. Suddenly my mate ran past us, followed by the Boss. 'Come on, Chippy, you shouldn't be up here,' said Hussey, and scooping

---

[103]Perhaps a (characteristically understated) reference to the near tragic mishap noted in the Introduction.

me up he accompanied me fore, where we found Blackborow. My fur was a little on end with all the confusion and the screaming of the ship and so forth, and it was very nice to have Blackborow stroke it down. He and I went below to the fo'c'sle, where I was placed upon his spare sweater. 'Best stay here, Chippy,' he said. 'No one knows what's happening from one moment to the next. You take charge of things here.' Kneaded his sweater with my paws, settling down after he left. It is the same old pattern of noise, shaking and then complete muddle. Dozed off and was awoken by Bakewell and How coming in and flopping down on their bunks as if tired. Woke again to find Bakewell and How gone, and Vincent and McCarthy flopping down on their beds. Speculating that this might go on all night, I burrowed more tightly into Blackborow's sweater, so as to ensure that I would not continue to be disturbed.

October 25th. Woke at dawn, with a sixth sense telling me that Ship Routine had been moved forward. Hurrying into the galley, arrived just as Cookie was leaving for the wardroom with a big pot of porridge. Led the way for him, just in front of his feet, meowing clearly so that he understood that I was there. A great cheer from my shipmates met us as we entered. Continued meowing as the porridge was ladled out to remind Cookie that I don't necessarily have to have porridge. 'Mrs Chippy!

What a nice surprise,' said Cheetham. 'Who told you breakfast was going to be four hours early?' I received rather a lot of attention from my shipmates,[104] before joining Cookie in the galley, where my own bowl was properly prepared with seal. My bowl empty, returned to the wardroom and began to clean my paws. Suddenly noticed that many of my shipmates were wet and dripping puddles on the floor, which I went over to examine, sniffing fastidiously at the unnecessary mess.[105] Looked up as half my shipmates shoved back their chairs and returned up top and the other half slumped over, falling asleep. Followed Bakewell as he trudged into the fo'c'sle and fell upon his bunk. Slept soundly until lunch, on account of having been up so early. Took my afternoon watch and observed blocks of ice as large as our ship flung into the air and then come down making a rather glorious splash of snow and ice. Strolled around on deck, but found everyone preoccupied and not very social. Returned to galley for snooze. Ship Routine maintained as usual, although rather

[104]See Note 102.
[105]Mrs Chippy's shipmates had worked through the night at the pumps trying to stem a dangerous leak that had sprung when the ship's stem had been savagely torn by the raging pressure of the ice. Mrs Chippy's mate, McNeish, had laboured in ice-cold water to build a cofferdam astern of the engines in an attempt to check the incoming flood of water. With virtually all hands so occupied, supervision of all the belowdecks – the galley, wardroom, stores and fo'c'sle – fell squarely on Mrs Chippy.

hurriedly. Slept in fo'c'sle on Blackborrow's berth.

October 26th. Woke in the night and found not everyone in their beds. It occurred to me that if my shipmates were indeed still awake, somebody might have seen that my bowl was empty and redressed this. Padded softly into galley and found this was not the case. Went into my cabin and found my mate's bed empty and uncrumpled, and decided to find him. Made my way to the forward hold and stopped some distance down the passage, listening to the clickety-clack of the pumps. Sniffed the air and observed that the area had lost all its pleasant musty mousiness and smelt rather salty and sea-ish. Continued cautiously towards flickering shadows in the entrance to the hold, and picking my way carefully around spots of wet and dampness looked down inside.

Observed my mate working busily below, hammering boards and nails and building a great wall. Lots of water was everywhere, running through the cracks in the wall, and peering down into the hold I saw my mate was standing almost to his waist in black water. Observed quietly at the head of the stairs for some time, then scratched the steps for attention. My mate looked up briefly and squinted towards me. Carefully settled on the step nearby in case he should be in need of my assistance. Dozed and was woken by the squelching of boots as my mate came up the stairs, while the Boss and Hurley were standing at the top of the staircase behind me. 'How did you manage?' asked the Boss, as my mate came towards him. My mate shrugged. 'It'll slow it, not stop it,' he said in his growly voice. 'The pumps will have to do the rest.' Bending down, he picked me up, as I was now standing near his boots. 'Good work,' said the Boss, clapping him on the shoulder as we wearily passed.[106] We both returned to our cabin and fell into bed, worn out. Slept late, waking just in time for breakfast and extracting myself from my mate's ankles made my way to the galley, where I found Blackborow and Cookie and my bowl filled. 'Well, Chippy, you seem to be holding up very well,' said Blackborow. I imagine the Boss had told them about how I was working until late last night. Found the wardroom almost deserted and strolled on deck. Sky very blue and warm, making for good visibility. Carefully selected first watch station and looked down onto the ice, where many of my shipmates were digging holes and trenches.[107] Observed fleecy clouds overhead and subtle, interesting ripple of ice. The ship was very noisy, making popping and creaking sounds throughout the day, which were distracting at first, but I soon tuned these out.[108] Lunch on deck for a change, which was

[106]McNeish had toiled at the cofferdam without break for twenty-eight hours.
[107]In a last desperate attempt to relieve the pressure.
[108]Shackleton recalled that on this day he could 'hear the creaking and groaning of [the *Endurance*'s] timbers, the pistol-like cracks that told of the starting of a trenail or plank, and the faint, indefinable whispers of our ship's distress' (Shackleton, *South*, pp. 73f.).

rather pleasant, taking advantage of the particularly good visibility. Tea in the wardroom quieter than usual as this new schedule seems to have made my shipmates rather less communicative. Joined my mate who was still in our cabin for a short snooze, waking just before dinner. 'Things are a bit rough just now, Chippy,' he said. 'We'll take it one thing at a time.' Purring my agreement, I accompanied my mate to the wardroom for dinner. Was enjoying a little after-dinner socializing when suddenly the ship started screaming so loudly none of us could hear ourselves speak. No one seemed at all surprised, though, and everyone just got up very slowly and trudged to the upper deck. A beautifully clear evening, not very dark. Dogs howling so loudly that the Boss had to shout orders to my shipmates above their annoying noise. Everyone started lowering things over the side onto the ice, doing a proper clear-out which is much needed after all the confusion over the past few days. Strolled onto the bridge, where the Skipper and Wild were chatting with the Boss. The Skipper looked as if he was going to cry, and I wondered if he was unwell. 'It will break her back,' he was saying, 'the ice is bending her like a bow.' The Boss patted him on the shoulder. 'Never did a more gallant ship –' the Skipper said, then broke off, as I wound around his boots. For some reason, the three of them burst out laughing. 'Chippy, Chippy,' said the Skipper. 'The indomitable Mrs Chippy.' Returned to deck and was just closing out my day with a final watch before going below, when ten penguins suddenly appeared on the floes beside us, more than I've ever seen together in all my watches. Observed them observe the ship. Then, as a group, they all threw back their heads and began to sing! All the fur on my back rose and my whiskers tingled. I arched up and bristled my tail while all my shipmates ran to the rail. 'Do you hear that?' McLeod said to Macklin. 'We'll none of us get back to our homes again.' Blackborow appeared some moments later, and took me with him belowdecks. 'Come on, Chippy,' he said. 'Let's get some sleep.' Accompanied Blackborow onto his bed, arranging myself on his pillow. Dreamed of the penguins and their song. None of the penguins I've ever observed before have looked particularly clever, yet these seemed to be trying to tell me something.[109]

October 27th. A most exciting day – perhaps the most exciting of our Expedition. I was taking a little snooze in the fo'c'sle with Bakewell and How shortly after teatime, when Wild stuck his head

[109]Interestingly, all of Mrs Chippy's shipmates were similarly affected by this strange interlude. Skipper Frank Worsley, for example, wrote of the penguins that '. . . I myself must confess that I have never, either before or since, heard them make any sound similar to the sinister wailings they moaned that day. I cannot explain the incident. But I don't mind admitting that it was one of the queerest, and also one of the most disquieting, things that had hitherto happened to me' (F. A. Worsley, *Endurance*, p. 16).

around the door and woke us. 'She's going, boys,' he said. 'I think it's time to get off.' Bakewell and How jumped up from their beds, and I stretched where I was on Blackborow's. 'Take my kit, will you?' Bakewell said to How. 'I'll get Chippy. Come on, Mrs Chips,' he said to me, and gently picked me up and tucked me under his arm. I was still somewhat asleep as we hurried up top, and so found everything rather confusing, with all my shipmates milling around the deck and going over the rail, and the dogs being unchained from their kennels. Suddenly I realized that Bakewell was taking me over the rail! I started to struggle and looking around I saw that everyone was leaving and that the ship was broken. The dogs were jumping and straining at the ends of their chains and it looked as if Bakewell was going to take me right past them. I won't say I was panicky but I was suddenly very concerned that he might not understand the exact nature and character of the dogs with respect to a sailor such as myself, how rude and aggressive they can be, and also there had been that little business of the kennel roofs and so forth. I began to struggle and he tried to hold me more tightly, talking all the time, but I had my eye on the dogs and wasn't entirely listening. 'Ow!' he exclaimed. 'Blast it! Chippy! Ow!' Then, 'Look! Here's your mate. Now everything will be all right.' I was still struggling to get clear and had made my way up to Bakewell's shoulder, when my mate came striding over to us and taking me firmly around the middle carried me over his head, back away from the crowd. 'There, there, little Chips,' he said. 'There, there,' and began to smooth down my fluffed-up fur. 'We're changing our quarters, that's all,' he said. 'Buck up now, and we'll soon be settled in.' Then holding me very firmly indeed, with one hand on my scruff, he strode towards the gangway. 'Have a last look, Chippy,' he said. 'We none of us will be back here again.'[110] The Boss was still standing on the poop deck giving orders as we walked quickly down the gangway, my mate holding me tightly against his sweater. And suddenly it was all over! We were on the ice! I began to look around and saw that we were leaving the dogs behind and making our way to what looked like a circle of large dogloos, but which are in fact tents set up not far from the ship. 'Here we are, Chippy,' said my mate, 'right as rain.' And stooping to his knees at the entrance of one of them, he put me inside. Relaxing my hold, I looked around and saw that it was very cosy, rather like when I burrow headfirst into a paper bag. My mate followed me inside, and unrolled a large piece of leather. 'Here's our sleeping bag, Chips,' he said. 'Reindeer skin, see, and' – he turned over a corner – 'it's got the fur inside.' My word, this was very luxurious! I sniffed the leather

[110]'Great spikes of ice were now forcing their way through the ship's sides. By degrees her head was getting more deeply buried . . . It was a heartbreaking sight to see the brave little ship, that had been our home for so long, broken up by the remorseless onward sweep of a thousand miles of pack-ice' (F. A. Worsley, *Endurance*, pp. 18f.).

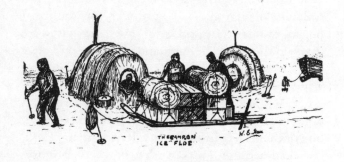

The camp on the ice floe.

carefully, finding it had a wonderfully rich, gamey tang, and began to knead it with my paws. 'There you go, Chippy,' said my mate. 'You're all set. Now stay here while I get back to the ship.' I continued to knead the soft leather and then carefully investigated the rather stiff fur on the inside. Purring loudly, I began to make my way a little deeper into the fur and was soon entirely concealed. Took a little snooze, so as to recover my energy for the next requirements of the Expedition and was awoken briefly by my mate putting a wooden board under our bag, and stowing some gear. Somewhat later, Wordie, McIlroy and last of all Wild crawled inside with us, each greeting me very warmly. 'Are you in our tent, Chippy?' McIlroy asked. 'Aren't we lucky!' Soon everyone was settled into his bag. 'Brr, it's cold,' said Wild. 'Chippy – sure you wouldn't like to sleep on my feet?' Briefly visited each of my tentmates in turn, purring loudly in their ears. Then settled down to sleep between my mate's ankles.

October 28th. Was awoken in the morning by Wild entering our tent with mugs of hot milk.[111] I arched my back, then walked up towards my

---

[111]The shipwrecked crew had to turn out of their tents three times in the course of their first night on the ice, due to cracking of the floe on which they were camped. Either these disruptions did not affect Mrs Chippy seriously enough to warrant mention in the Journal, or Mrs Chippy may have slept through them.

mate's head, stretching each leg as I went, while my mate poured a little something from his mug into my bowl. Reflected as I had my milk that this was a promising start to a new routine. After breakfast, cleaned my paws and whiskers on our bag while listening to my tentmates groan about how cold and stiff they were etc. etc. and how they hadn't got much sleep due to the grinding noise of the ice. In fact, if properly used, these reindeer bags are more comfortable than our Ship berths. The ice noises are very distracting to be sure, but I found that by purring I managed to drown them out. Eventually, everyone crawled out of his bag and went outside, leaving me in the tent. 'I'd stay here, if I was you, Chippy,' said my mate. 'No need going out in the cold.' Settling on our bag to clean, I noticed how very warm the fur was inside and decided to investigate if it was warm all the way down to the bottom. Dozed briefly, waking with the conviction that it must be nearly lunchtime. Cautiously put my head outside our tent, and observed my shipmates bustling to and fro. Came out a little further and caught sight of other tents next to ours. Carefully testing the ice with my paw, I found it cold but not unpleasant and no different than the snow and ice that fell on our ship's deck. Sniffing the air, I ascertained that the dogs were safely housed some distance away and took a little stroll towards a cloud of black and rather oily-smelling smoke I happened to have noticed at the edge of the tents and which, as I discovered, led to

The makeshift galley on the ice floe.

Cookie. 'Well, well, look who's turned up!' said Cookie, seeing me standing at his feet. He was stirring something in a black pot on top of a smoking stove. I considered it my duty to acquaint myself with Camp Routine as soon as possible, and informed Cookie by meowing that this was the case. Was greeted by Blackborow, who was carrying some boxes over to the stove. 'Chippy, well I never,' he said. 'So you've found the new galley.' Remained with my old friends in the galley as they continued to cut things up and stir them in the pot. Presently, we were joined by my shipmates, who gathered in a half circle in front of the galley holding their bowls. Enjoyed a hot lunch with my shipmates and at my mate's urging accompanied him back to our tent, where I settled on the reindeer bag and my shipmates' new woolly jerseys.[112] 'Chippy seems to be managing well enough,' said Wordie, who was putting his new sweater inside the tent, 'as usual.' Took a little snooze and awoke towards teatime, ready to go on camp patrol. Determined to familiarize

ENDURANCE

myself with our camp, I conducted a brief investigation of the other tents, just poking my head inside for a moment or two, examining the other reindeer

[112]Shackleton had issued new winter clothing to all hands.

bags and stones. Walked cautiously back towards the galley and made a detour close to where our ship lay level with the ice, its masts all broken, my watch rail crumpled and all the ropes I used to play with tangled. Stood looking at it, briefly recalling the mouse holds, and the Ritz stove and my potato pot. Shifted my attention to my shipmates who were stacking up crates and boxes around our new galley. Seeing that everyone was occupied, took a little stroll closer to where the dogs were being kept, just to see what arrangements had been made here. Observed them closely and ascertained that although they were without kennels, they were firmly chained. Strolling a little closer, I remarked that they were looking rather woebegone, all frosty and uncouth. Strolled a little closer, ignoring raucous din, and seeing a piece of loose ice, scampered after it, casually bowling it along in front of them. Stopped and admired the view, sniffing the air and looking to the horizon. Bowled the ice along again, then strolled back towards the galley. Observed from the corner of my eye Macklin and Wild running towards the dogs as I was leaving. 'Now what's set them off?' Macklin was shouting as he ran. 'They've been nothing but trouble!' Appeared at Cookie's feet in galley. 'Like clockwork,' said Cookie to me, shaking his head. Shortly afterwards my shipmates gathered again at the galley, and we all received our tea. Accompanied my mate back to our tent, thinking to myself that I've more or less got the hang of Camp Routine. Snoozed on reindeer bag until dinner, which we had in the entrance to our tents. My shipmates are not as jolly as they were and do not seem to have adapted as readily as I have to the new schedule. Joined my mate on a constitutional stroll around the tents. Just as we had reached the last tent and were turning back, I happened to notice some interesting shadows flickering inside. Creeping closer, I crouched by the tent wall so as to focus on the shadow movement. Continued to monitor the movement, then suddenly pounced, making a very satisfactory connection with the movement and bringing it to a stop. 'Something's outside!' Lees's voice yelled from behind the tent cloth. Out popped Clark and Blackborow, looking around them, and then both burst out laughing, along with my mate. 'What is it?' called Lees, very anxiously. 'It's a seal,' Clark called back. 'A big one.' 'Hello, Mrs Chippy. What do you think of the new camp?' said Blackborow, stooping to pick me up. 'Have a look inside?' In fact I already had, but my mate and I accepted the invitation and passed a very sociable hour, talking about this and that and testing all the bags. Returning with my mate to our tent, I had another scamper over the ice, apprehending chunks of snow and such, looking in holes before bounding into our tent. Found all my tentmates in their bags, chatting. Settled between my mate's ankles and reflected how satisfying it was to have explored the ice and to know that it was nothing particularly difficult to manage, and how jolly the Expedition had become.

The end.

October 29th. Slept very deeply, but woke in the night and relocated to inside my mate's bag, settling on his chest. 'Chippy, you're better than a water bottle,' he said, stroking me very comfortably. 'I'll take Chippy next, if you get too hot,' said Wild, in the darkness. 'Chippy, my bag's nice and toasty,' called McIlroy. It seemed everyone was awake. Purred myself to sleep, listening to my tentmates' invitations. Was awoken in the morning by McIlroy coming into the tent with all our breakfast bowls. My word, this new routine is working splendidly! While my tentmates went outside, returned to the furry part of my bag to clean my paws and whiskers. Stretched and prepared to make my camp patrol. Stepped outside and observed that my shipmates were all mustered in the centre of the tents and strolled over to join them. Found them all standing very solemnly to attention, listening to the Boss. 'But if you keep your spirits up and give me your loyalty, we'll all get home,' he was saying. These were proper expeditionary words and as my shipmates cheered, I wound around their ankles, indicating my complete support. The Boss contin-ued to explain that we would shortly begin our Imperial walk towards the nearest land, and that we must ruthlessly strip our possessions to the barest minimum.[113] 'The value of everything you carry must be weighed against your survival,' he said. 'Anything that cannot pull its weight or is not

[113]Shackleton hoped to lead the men to Paulet Island, some 346 miles away.

useful to the Expedition must be put down.' My word, this was rather stiff! Luckily I have only my bowl and blanket and my mate will see to those. Meanwhile the Boss took some gold coins out of his jacket and put them down in the snow, by way of example. Then he held up his big Bible and tearing out some pages to keep, he put it down beside the coins.[114] After he left, I made my way over to the coins and carefully examined them, then tested the Bible with the tip of my paw. Suddenly I looked up and saw all my shipmates gathered round me, looking very disconsolate. Clark stooped and picked me up and began to stroke me. I expect he's thinking of all those nets and bottles he will have to leave behind. As the Boss knows, I am like him, never downcast, and I can see that from now on I will have to exert all my leadership skills to buck everyone up. 'Chippy, we're glad you shipped on,' said Bakewell. My mate came over very slowly, and my shipmates parted and Clark handed me to him. I was stroked again as he held me, then he turned and walked very slowly towards our tent. We had just settled inside, when I heard a crunching on the ice and then Black-borow poked his head inside, looking rather pasty

---

[114]The pages that Shackleton retained were those containing the Twenty-third Psalm and this verse from the Book of Job:
> Out of whose womb came the ice?
> And the hoary frost of Heaven, who hath gendered it?
> The waters are hid as with a stone.
> And the face of the deep is frozen.

and pale. 'I brought this,' he said, showing my bowl to my mate. 'From Cookie and me.' My mate rose to his knees and, clapping Blackborow on the shoulder, stepped outside. 'Here, little Chippy,' said Blackborow. Addressing myself to my bowl, I discovered it had been prepared with sardines! And properly speaking, it wasn't really a meal time! Purring loudly as I ate, I reflected that we should have got this Expedition under way long ago, instead of sitting around on the ship. Finished my bowl and saw that Blackborow was in a sociable mood, very willing to have a proper stroke and head rub, i.e., first on top, then on each side, then under my chin, and a little chat. He stroked me for a long time as I sat beside him on the reindeer bag, then my mate drew back the flap and looked at us. Blackborow picked me up and held me tightly against his cheek. 'Chippy,' he said, then he put me down and left. Purring, I made my way to my mate and settled comfortably on his lap. 'Sardines, was it, Chippy?' he said. 'That was a treat.' I stretched out along his knees while he stroked me. 'The crew are all glad you shipped along,' he said suddenly, 'every man of them.' I think he was feeling a bit homesick after all our moving around and so on, for he began to recall all the places we've been and the things we've done together, the cottage in Cathcart and the vegetable garden, and playing with his daughter. I purred and kneaded his knees occasionally for emphasis, also recalling one or two things he may

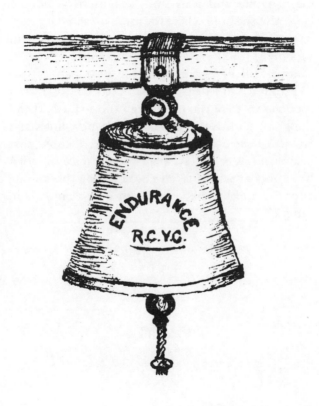

not have known, i.e., the dustbin behind Mrs McPhearson's house, and the squirrel nest in the young oak tree. 'We've seen the world, you and I, Chippy,' he said, and recalled the sea and the ice, the penguins and seals and the butterfly-coloured city. Also the hold where the mice are and the galley stove and our old berth. I purred in agreement, becoming rather drowsy. Observance of strict routine will be essential for the next part of our Expedition and I began to plan accordingly. First a little snooze to regain my energy and so forth, then I think an examination of those little paw holes and crevices I see everywhere in the ice. I know that Clark and Wordie say there are no mice or voles here, but the Scientists have been wrong about quite a lot else and I think a thorough investigation is in order.[115]

[115]This is the last entry in Mrs Chippy's Journal. As is well known, on 30 August 1916, after many months of hardship, Shackleton secured the rescue of all his men.